Pflichtmaterialien Abitur Niedersachsen 2022

Cornelsen

Contents

Abbreviations and symbols

adj	adjective
f./ff.	and the following page(s)/line(s)
fml	formal
infml	informal
jdn., jdm.	*jemanden, jemandem*
l., ll.	line, lines
n	noun
p., pp.	page, pages
pl	plural
sb.	somebody
sl	slang
sth.	something
v	verb

cornelsen.de
Code: xxxxx

The webcode can be entered at www.cornelsen.de to connect you directly to a website with additional material.

Module I

World in Transit

Part A
Pre-reading activities

3 refuge ['refjuːdʒ]: place where you are protected from danger
7 hostile: mean and aggressive
13 tormentor [tɔː'mentə] (fml): person who causes sb. to suffer

A1 'Distant Shore' *Billy Bragg and The Blokes*

Read the following song text and complete the tasks on p. 6.

Everyone knows
That there's no place like home
But I'm just seeking refuge
In a world full of storms
Washed up on a distant shore
Can't go home anymore

The natives are hostile
Whatever I say
The thing they fear most is
That I might want to stay
By their side on a distant shore
Can't go home anymore

I escape my tormentors
By crossing the sea
What I cannot escape is
Memory
Far away on a distant shore
Can't go home anymore

Singer/songwriter Billy Bragg performing onstage

From: Union Prod. Ltd./Musik Edition Discoton, Berlin/Sony/ATV Music Publishing (Germany) GmbH, Berlin/Billy Bragg

Comprehension

1 a Writing Write a short biography of the (imaginary) speaker of the song text (→ Info box, p. 97). Consider the following points:
- where the speaker comes from;
- what the speaker has experienced in the past;
- where the speaker is now (and for what reason);
- how the speaker feels about their present situation.

b Compare biographies with a partner. Discuss the points on which you disagree.

Analysis

2 a Discuss with your partner what music style you think the song has.

b Find the song on the internet and listen to it.

c Assess the style of the song and whether or not it fits the message.

3 The word 'distant' normally refers to a place that is far away from the speaker. Explain how the word is used here and discuss why it is repeated so often.

Beyond the text

4 The song originally came out in 2002. Discuss whether or not it is still relevant today.

5 Writing Your group is making a video clip for an online forum on the situation of refugees. You must decide whether or not to use the song 'Distant Shore' as background music. Write a comment in which you name reasons for your decision.

Refugees and migrants arrive in Lesbos, Greece, on 11 October 2015, after crossing the Aegean Sea on a boat from Turkey.

A2 Working with a painting

Take a look at the painting *UK School Report* by Tam Joseph and complete the tasks that follow.

1 a Form groups of four. Put a large sheet of paper in the middle of your group. Each of you has one corner of the page to write in.
  b Make notes on your first reaction to the picture in your corner of the placemat.
  c After two minutes, rotate the paper 90° and comment (in writing) on what you can now read in your partner's corner.
  d After two more minutes (or when everyone has finished writing), rotate the paper and comment again. Continue until you have your original remarks in front of you again.
  e Read what the other three members of your group have added to your first reaction.
2 Describe the picture. Pay close attention to details (similarities and differences). Make notes in the table below.

Similarities	Differences

3 Relate the title of the picture to its content.
4 **Writing** Imagine you are a teacher at a British school. You have known the student portrayed in the picture for many years and have observed his development. The student is now facing disciplinary measures for misbehaviour. Write a report to the head teacher in which you summarize your observations of the student's personal development and the reasons for it.
5 Your class is preparing a presentation on 'Bias and Race'. Your task is to find suitable visual material. Assess the picture at hand with regard to its suitability.

A3 People in motion *Paul Maloney*

Read the following text about migration and complete the tasks on pp. 9–11.

From the beginning of human history, people and peoples have been on the move. The decline of the Roman Empire was accompanied by a mass migration of Germanic tribes that radically changed the face of Europe. Centuries later, the age of discovery and exploration paved the way for colonialism and mass emigration to the so-called 'New World'.

Today we distinguish between different forms of migration based on motives and circumstances. Immigrants, for example, leave their home country more or less voluntarily, and in most cases they migrate to a particular country with the intention of becoming citizens of their new country of residence. The word 'migrant' is generally used to refer to migrant workers who leave home temporarily in order to find work. The money sent home by migrant workers to their families is often an important economic factor in developing countries.

Many of those who live outside their home country have not migrated voluntarily. Asylum seekers, for example, are people who have fled from persecution in their country of origin. Many countries grant asylum to those who are persecuted for political or religious reasons. Other people flee to escape catastrophes (e.g. droughts). Such people are known as refugees. The rights of refugees and the obligations of member states to provide humanitarian aid are regulated in the 1951 Refugee Convention of the UN. People (usually belonging to a certain ethnic group) who are expelled from their country of residence (for example as the result of a lost war) are referred to as displaced persons (e.g. German nationals who formerly lived in Eastern European countries and were forced to emigrate after World War II).

The factors that influence global migration can be divided into push factors and pull factors. Push factors are those that drive people to run for their lives or to try their luck elsewhere: violence, corruption, poverty, natural disasters, lack of perspective. Pull factors are those that make countries look attractive to prospective immigrants: political stability, economic opportunity, tolerance, rule of law, democracy. In extreme cases, refugees fleeing from hopelessness are willing to risk everything (including their lives) for the vague hope of a better life abroad.

The total number of people living outside their country of origin has reached an all-time high and is growing faster than the world population. In addition to international migration there is also internal migration. This is, for example, when people are forced to leave their traditional homeland for another region within their own country. A number of fairly recent developments have contributed to the worldwide rise in migration. Globalization is one of them: in a globalized economy, skilled labour migrates to the country that offers the highest wages. The internet as a worldwide medium of communication has made it easier for people to obtain information on job opportunities in other countries. Another factor is the rise of English as an international lingua franca (a legacy of the British Empire). Finally, the availability of moderately priced air travel has made the world labour market more mobile than ever before.

Those who move permanently to a different country with the intention of making it their home are usually expected to integrate to a certain degree. Integration can include, for example, learning the language of the country, applying for citizenship, and respecting the norms of public behaviour. At the same time, immigrants often wish to retain at least part of their ethnic identity. This identity can manifest itself in matters of religion, language, dress and food, but also in family structures and social attitudes. For this reason, immigrants from the same country tend to form ethnic communities within the larger society in which they live. Successful integration ultimately requires good will, tolerance and mutual respect from both the new arrivals and the society they wish to be included in. Tensions may also arise within the community, for example between first-generation immigrants and their children, who often have a stronger sense of attachment to their new homeland and reject the ways of their parents as irrelevant and outmoded.

From: 2019, unpublished manuscript

1 Match the English term to its German equivalent:

asylum seeker
country of origin
country of residence
displaced persons
immigrant
internal migration
lingua franca
natural disaster
migrant worker
persecution
skilled labour
rule of law

Wanderarbeiter/in
Aufenthaltsland
Binnenmigration
Verfolgung
Vertriebene
Einwanderer/-in
Rechtsstaatlichkeit
Naturkatastrophe
Fachkräfte
Verkehrssprache
Asylbewerber/in
Herkunftsland

2 Complete the sentences below with a word chosen from one of the boxes (verbs must be put in the right form):

aid | factors | economic | ethnic | grant | mutual | origin | citizenship | seek | flee

A The German government ______________________ asylum to people who are persecuted in their home country.

B Many skilled workers come to Western countries ______________________ employment.

C War and natural disasters are among the most common ______________________ that drive people away from their homes.

D Most immigrants apply for ______________________ in their new country of residence.

E UN member states are required to offer refugees some form of humanitarian

______________________.

F Millions of refugees ______________________ from the prolonged drought in East Africa.

G US cities have long had ______________________ neighbourhoods such as Chinatown or Little Italy.

H Indonesia and the Philippines are major countries of ______________________ of migrant workers.

I Integration can only succeed as the result of ______________________ effort.

J America attracted millions of immigrants with the promise of political freedom and

______________________ opportunity.

3 a Complete the table below with the missing forms. Use a dictionary if necessary.

verb	noun (person)	(abstract) noun	adjective
apply	applicant		
attract	—		
immigrate			—
	influencer		
	—		mobile
			motivational
originate	—		
		persecution	—
—		politics	
respect	—		
	—		tolerant
			voluntary

b Choose five of the words you have added to the table in **a** and use each of them in a sentence.

A ______________________________.

B ______________________________.

C ______________________________.

D ______________________________.

E ______________________________.

A4 Working with a world map

1 Find the following countries on the map and label them: Brazil, Egypt, England, France, Hungary, India, Iraq, Pakistan, Saudi Arabia, Somalia, Spain, Syria, the Caribbean / West Indies, Turkey, Uganda, USA, Uzbekistan.

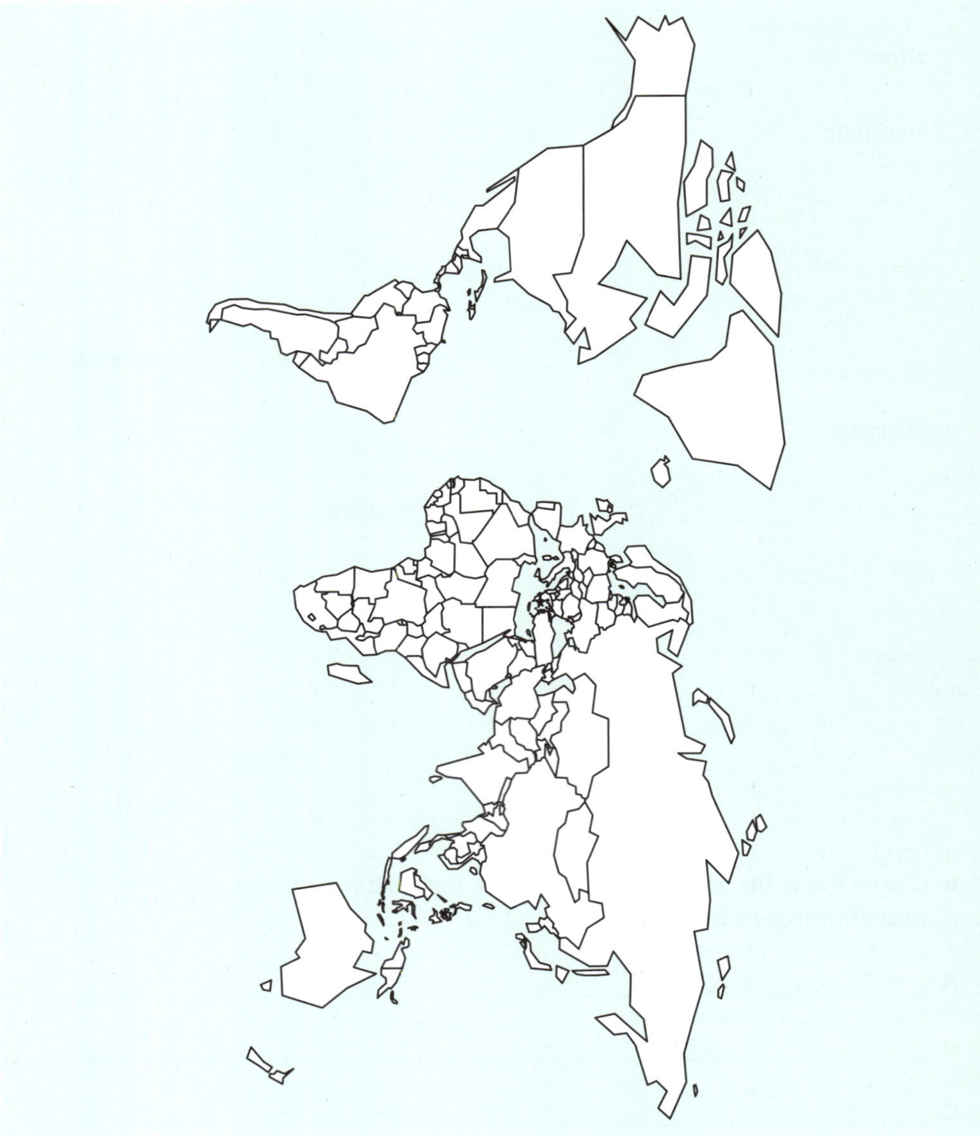

2 a Why do you think you were asked to find these specific countries?

b Find out if they are a former British colony (or protectorate). If so, colour them in blue.

Part B
While-reading activities

B1 'Loose Change' *Andrea Levy*

1 What are your first associations when you hear 'Loose Change'? Take notes and compare your ideas with a partner.

2 The following are the first two sentences from the short story you are about to read.

I'm not in the habit of making friends with strangers. I'm a Londoner.

Imagine the kind of person the protagonist could be. Write down three sentences about your idea of him/her.

A ______________________________

B ______________________________

C ______________________________

Read the short story 'Loose Change' by Andrea Levy and complete the tasks on pp. 19–21.

I am not in the habit of making friends of strangers. I'm a Londoner. Not even little grey-haired old ladies passing comment on the weather can shame a response from me. I'm a Londoner – aloof sweats from my pores. But I was in a bit of a predicament; my period was two days early and I was caught unprepared.

I'd just gone into the National Portrait Gallery to get out of the cold. It had begun to feel, as I'd walked through the bleak streets, like acid was being thrown at my exposed skin. My fingers were numb, searching in my purse for change for the tampon machine; I barely felt the pull of the zip. But I didn't have any coins. I was forced to ask in a loud voice in this small lavatory, 'Has anyone got three twenty-pence pieces?'

Everyone seemed to leave the place at once – all of them Londoners I was sure of it. Only she was left – fixing her hair in the mirror.

'Do you have change?'

She turned round slowly as I held out a ten-pound note. She had the most spectacular eyebrows. I could see the lines of black hair, like magnetised iron filings, tumbling across her eyes and almost joining above her nose. I must have been staring to recall them so clearly. She had wide black eyes and a round face with such a solid jawline that

1 habit: usual behaviour
3 aloof: (being) not interested in other people
4 predicament [prɪˈdɪkəmənt]: difficult situation
7 bleak: empty, cold
8 numb: unable to feel anything
11 lavatory [ˈlævətri] (fml): room with a toilet
17 tumble (v): fall suddenly
18 recall sth.: remember sth.
19 jawline: chin

she looked to have taken a gentle whack from Tom and Jerry's cartoon frying pan. She dug into the pocket of her jacket and pulled out a bulging handful of money. It was coppers mostly. Some of it tinkled on to the floor. But she had change: too much – I didn't want a bag full of the stuff myself.

'Have you a five-pound note as well?' I asked.

She dropped the coins on to the basin area, spreading them out into the soapy puddles of water that were lying there. Then she said, 'You look?' She had an accent but I couldn't tell then where it was from; I thought maybe Spain.

'Is this all you've got?' I asked. She nodded. 'Well, look, let me just take this now …' I picked three damp coins out of the pile. 'Then I'll get some change in the shop and pay them back to you.' Her gaze was as keen as a cat with string. 'Do you understand? Only I don't want all those coins.'

'Yes,' she said softly.

I was grateful. I took the money. But when I emerged from the cubicle the girl and her handful of change were gone.

I found her again staring at the portrait of Darcy Bussell. Her head was inclining from one side to the other as if the painting were a dress she might soon try on for size. I approached her about the money but she just said, 'This is good picture.' Was it my explanation left dangling or the fact that she liked the dreadful painting that caused my mouth to gape?

'Really, you like it?' I said.

'She doesn't look real. It looks like …' Her eyelids fluttered sleepily as she searched for the right word, 'a dream.'

That particular picture always reminded me of the doodles girls drew in their rough books at school.

'You don't like?' she asked. I shrugged. 'You show me one you like,' she said.

As I mentioned before, I'm not in the habit of making friends of strangers, but there was something about this girl. Her eyes were encircled with dark shadows so that even when she smiled – introducing herself cheerfully as Laylor – they remained as mournful as a glum kid at a party. I took this fraternisation as defeat but I had to introduce her to a better portrait.

Alan Bennett with his mysterious little brown bag didn't impress her at all. She preferred the photograph of Beckham. Germaine Greer made her top lip curl and as for A. S. Byatt, she laughed out loud, 'This is child make this?'

We were almost making a scene. Laylor couldn't keep her voice down and people were beginning to watch us. I wanted to be released from my obligation. 'Look, let me buy us both a cup of tea,' I said. 'Then I can give you back your money.'

20 whack (n): act of hitting sb./sth.
22 coppers (pl): coins of low value
22 tinkle (v): make a light sound

32 gaze (n): long, steady look, stare
36 emerge: come out of
38 Darcey Bussell (born 1969): British retired ballerina, who went on to have a career in TV
39 incline (v, fml): bend
41 dangle: *baumeln (lassen)*
44 gape (v): fall open
47 doodle (n): *Kritzelei*
49 shrug (v): *mit den Achseln zucken*
54 mournful [ˈmɔːnfl]: very sad
55 glum: sad, quiet
55 fraternisation [ˌfrætənaɪˈzeɪʃn]: *Verbrüderung*
57 Alan Bennett (born 1934): English actor and author
58 David Beckham (born 1975): retired English football star
58 Germaine Greer (born 1939): Australian scholar and feminist writer
59 A. S. Byatt [ˈbaɪət] (born 1936): pen name of Dame Antonia Susan Duffy, English novelist and poet
63 obligation [ˌɒblɪˈgeɪʃn]: duty

She brought out her handful of change again as we sat down at a table – eagerly passing it across to me to take some for the tea.

'No, I'll get this,' I said.

Her money jangled like a win on a slot machine as she tipped it back into her pocket. When I got back with the tea, I pushed over the twenty-pences I owed her. She began playing with them on the tabletop pushing one around the other two in a figure of eight. Suddenly she leant towards me as if there were a conspiracy between us and said, 'I like art,' With that announcement a light briefly came on in those dull eyes to reveal that she was no more than eighteen. A student perhaps.

'Where are you from?' I asked.

'Uzbekistan,' she said.

Was that the Balkans? I wasn't sure. 'Where is that?'

She licked her finger, then with great concentration drew an outline on to the tabletop. 'This is Uzbekistan,' she said. She licked her finger again to carefully plop a wet dot on to the map saying, 'And I come from here – Tashkent.'

'And where is all this?' I said, indicating the area around the little map with its slowly evaporating borders and town. She screwed up her face as if to say nowhere.

'Are you on holiday?' I asked.

She nodded.

'How long are you here for?'

Leaning her elbows on the table she took a sip of her tea, 'Ehh, it is bitter!' she shouted.

'Put some sugar in it,' I said, pushing the sugar sachets toward her.

She was reluctant, 'Is for free?' she asked.

'Yes, take one.'

The sugar spilled as she clumsily opened the packet. I laughed it off but she, with the focus of a prayer, put her cup up to the edge of the table and swept the sugar into it with the side of her hand. The rest of the detritus that was on the tabletop fell into the tea as well. Some crumbs, a tiny scrap of paper and a curly black hair floated on the surface of her drink. I felt sick as she put the cup back to her mouth.

'Pour that one away, I'll get you another one.'

Just as I said that a young boy arrived at our table and stood, legs astride, before her. He pushed down the hood on his padded coat. His head was curious – flat as a cardboard cut-out – with hair stuck to his sweaty forehead in black curlicues. And his face was as doggedly determined as two fists raised. They began talking in whatever language it was they spoke. Laylor's tone pleading – the boy's aggrieved. Laylor took the money from her pocket and held it up to him. She slapped his hand away when he tried to wrest all the coins from her palm. Then, as abruptly as he had appeared, he left. Laylor called something after him. Everyone turned to stare at her, except the boy, who just carried on.

68 jangle (v): klirren
68 slot machine: *Spielautomat*
70 owe sb. sth. [əʊ]: have to pay back money that you borrowed
72 conspiracy [kənˈspɪrəsi]: secret plan
73 dull: boring
80 dot: small round mark
83 evaporate [ɪˈvæpəreɪt]: disappear
83–84 screw up one's face (infml): *das Gesicht verziehen*
90 sachet [ˈsæʃeɪ]: small paper package
91 reluctant [rɪˈlʌktənt]: hesitant
93 clumsy: not elegant
96 detritus [dɪˈtraɪtəs] (fml): pieces of waste
101 astride [əˈstraɪd]: apart
103–104 doggedly determined: very determined
105 plead: *bitten, flehen*
105 aggrieved: *gekränkt*
106 slap sth. away: *etwas wegschlagen*
107 wrest sth.: *etwas entreißen*

'Who was that?'

With the teacup resting on her lip, she said, 'My brother. He want to know where we sleep tonight.'

'Oh, yes, where's that?' I was rummaging through the contents of my bag for a tissue, so it was casually asked.

'It's square we have slept before.'

'Which hotel is it?' I thought of the Russell Hotel, that was on a square with uniformed attendants, bed turning-down facilities, old-world style.

She was picking the curly black hair off her tongue when she said, 'No hotel, just the square.'

It was then I began to notice things I had not seen before: dirt under each of her chipped fingernails, the collar of her blouse crumpled and unironed, a tiny cut on her cheek, a fringe that looked to have been cut with blunt nail-clippers. I found a tissue and used it to wipe my sweating palms.

'How do you mean just in the square?'

'We sleep out in the square,' she said. It was so simple she spread her hands to suggest the lie of her bed.

'Outside?'

She nodded.

'Tonight?'

'Yes.'

The memory of the bitter cold still tingled at my fingertips as I said, 'Why?' It took her no more than two breaths to tell me the story. She and her brother had had to leave their country, Uzbekistan, when their parents, who were journalists, were arrested. It was arranged very quickly – friends of their parents acquired passports for them and put them on to a plane. They had been in England for three days but they knew no one here. This country was just a safe place. Now all the money they had could be lifted in the palm of a hand to a stranger in a toilet. So they were sleeping rough – in the shelter of a square, covered in blankets, on top of some cardboard.

At the next table a woman was complaining loudly that there was too much froth on her coffee. Her companion was relating the miserable tale of her daughter's attempt to get into publishing. What did they think about the strange girl sitting opposite me? Nothing. Only I knew what a menacing place Laylor's world had become. She'd lost a tooth. I noticed the ugly gap when she smiled at me saying, 'I love London.'

She had sought me out – sifted me from the crowd. This young woman was desperate for help. She'd even cunningly made me obliged to her.

'I have picture of Tower Bridge at home on wall although I have not seen yet.'

113 rummage through sth. [ˈrʌmɪdʒ]: *etwas durchstöbern*
114 tissue [ˈtɪʃuː]: paper handkerchief
117 attendant [əˈtendənt]: person who serves in a hotel
122 chipped: *eingerissen, abgebrochen*
123 fringe (n): front part of sb's hair
124 blunt: not sharp
124 nail-clippers (pl): tool for cutting one's nails
133 tingle: *kribbeln*
141 sleep rough: be homeless
144 froth [frɒθ]: *Schaum*
147 menacing [ˈmenəsɪŋ]: threatening
149 sift sth./sb.: *etwas/jdn. aussieben*
150 cunning: *raffiniert, gerissen*
150 obliged to sb. [əˈblaɪdʒd] *jdm. verpflichtet (sein)*

But why me? I had my son to think of. Why pick on a single mother with a young son? We haven't got the time. Those two women at the next table, with their matching handbags and shoes, they did nothing but lunch. Why hadn't she approached them instead?

'From little girl, I always want to see it …' she went on.

I didn't know anything about people in her situation. Didn't they have to go somewhere? Croydon, was it? Couldn't she have gone to the police? Or some charity? My life was hard enough without this stranger tramping through it. She smelt of mildewed washing. Imagine her dragging that awful stink into my kitchen. Cupping her filthy hands round my bone china. Smearing my white linen. Her big face with its pantomime eyebrows leering over my son. Slumping on to my sofa and kicking off her muddy boots as she yanked me down into her particular hell. How would I ever get rid of her?

'You know where is Tower Bridge?'

Perhaps there was something tender-hearted in my face. When my grandma first came to England from the Caribbean she lived through days as lonely and cold as an open grave. The story she told all her grandchildren was about the stranger who woke her while she was sleeping in a doorway and offered her a warm bed for the night. It was this act of benevolence that kept my grandmother alive. She was convinced of it. Her Good Samaritan.

'Is something wrong?' the girl asked.

Now my grandmother talks with passion about scrounging refugees; those asylum seekers who can't even speak the language, storming the country and making it difficult for her and everyone else.

'Last week …' she began, her voice quivering, 'I was in home.' This was embarrassing. I couldn't turn the other way, the girl was staring straight at me. 'This day, Friday,' she went on, 'I cooked fish for my mother and brother.' The whites of her eyes were becoming soft and pink; she was going to cry. 'This day Friday I am here in London,' she said. 'And I worry I will not see my mother again.'

Only a savage would turn away when it was merely kindness that was needed. I resolved to help her. I had three warm bedrooms, one of them empty. I would make her dinner. Fried chicken or maybe poached fish in wine. I would run her a bath filled with bubbles. Wrap her in thick towels heated on a rail. I would then hunt out some warm clothes and after I had put my son to bed I would make her cocoa. We would sit and talk. I would let her tell me all that she had been through. Wipe her tears and assure her that she was now safe. I would phone a colleague from school and ask him for advice. Then in the morning I would take Laylor to wherever she needed to go. And before we said goodbye I would press my phone number into her hand.

160 Croydon: area in South London
162 mildewed [ˈmɪldjuːd]: *schimmelig, muffig*
163 cup your hands around sth.: hold sth. in your hands
163 filthy: very dirty
164 bone china: fine porcelain
164 linen [ˈlɪnɪn]: bed sheets
165 leer over sb.: give evil looks to sb.
165 slump (v): sit or fall down heavily
166 yank sb.: pull sb. hard
167 get rid of sb.: *jdn. loswerden*
169 tender-hearted: kind
174 benevolence [bəˈnevələns]: kind, helpful feeling
175 Samaritan [səˈmærɪtən]: *Samariter/in*
177 scrounge [skraʊndʒ] (v): *schnorren, betteln*
180 quiver [ˈkwɪvə] (v): shake
186 savage [ˈsævɪdʒ] (n): wild, cruel person
187 resolve to do [rɪˈzɒlv] (fml): make a decision to do
193 assure sb. (that) …: tell sb. that sth. is definitely true

All Laylor's grandchildren would know my name. Her nose was running with snot. She pulled down the sleeve of her jacket to drag it across her face and said, 'I must find my brother.'

I didn't have any more tissues. 'I'll get you something to wipe your nose,' I said.

I got up from the table. She watched me, frowning; the tiny hairs of her eyebrows locking together like Velcro. I walked to the counter where serviettes were lying in a neat pile. I picked up four. Then standing straight I walked on. Not back to Laylor but up the stairs to the exit. I pushed through the revolving doors and threw myself into the cold.

From: Maggie Hamand (publisher): Underwords: The Hidden City. *London: Maia Press, 2005, pp. 67–76*

198 drag sth.: pull sth. with effort
203 Velcro: *Klettverschluss*
206 revolving door: *Drehtür*

Info Andrea Levy
Prizewinning author Andrea Levy (1956–2019) was born and raised on a North London council estate. She was of Black, Scottish and Jewish heritage. Her father came to England from Jamaica in 1948 with the first wave of immigrants on the Empire Windrush ship, and her mother followed six months later on a banana boat. Levy first studied textile design and became a costume assistant for the Royal Opera and the BBC. She then founded a graphic design company. She only started writing in her mid-thirties after joining a creative writing class. Her most famous novel was the enormously successful *Small Island* (2004), which was adapted for television (BBC) and theatre (National Theatre London). Levy's main literary subjects were the legacy of the British Empire, racism in post-war Britain and slavery in the Caribbean. She fought to have the largely forgotten impact of slavery be taught in UK schools. Through her writing she wanted to encourage conversations about British colonial and post-colonial history and national identity.

Info Uzbekistan

The Republic of Uzbekistan is a small country in Central Asia. Its capital is Tashkent. Formerly a part of the Soviet Union, it declared its independence in 1991. Uzbekistan first struggled with the legacy of communism. The government was internationally criticized for human rights abuses. In May 2005 the military opened fire on a large group of protestors in the city of Andijon and hundreds of people died. Additionally, Islamic militant groups attempted to gain ground, which led to further outbreaks of violence and persecution of Muslims. The Uzbekistan state has also used forced labour for their cotton industry. After the death of long-term president Islam Karimov in 2016, the country slowly started to introduce a few, mainly economically motivated reforms.

Comprehension

3 Give short answers to the following questions:

A Where is the short story set?

____

B Which problem does the narrator have at the beginning of the story?

____

C What is the other woman's reaction when the narrator asks her for change?

____

D What does the narrator want to do after picking three coins, and why?

____

E Why does the young woman like the portrait of Darcy Bussell?

____

F Why does the narrator feel uncomfortable when looking at portraits with Laylor?

____

G What does the narrator know about Uzbekistan?

____

H What does Laylor's brother want, and why is he angry?

____

I Look at ll. 113–132. What does the narrator realize at this point?

____

J Look at ll. 143–167. What does the narrator worry about?

____

K What do we learn about the narrator's grandmother?

____

L Look at ll. 186–196. What does the narrator decide to do and why?

____

4 Outline the reasons why Laylor came to London
5 List all the (unwritten) rules the narrator seems to follow in her life. e.g. *Don't talk to strangers*.
6 Summarize the narrator's dilemma.

Analysis

7 a The elements listed in the table below can be regarded as characteristic of most short stories. Check if these elements are present in 'Loose Change'.

Feature	'Loose Change'
A length (can be read in one sitting)	
B direct start	
C limited number of characters	
D concentration on one character/situation/dilemma/problem	
E focus on one single aspect which undergoes a change in the course of the story	

b Based on what you found in **a**, would you classify 'Loose Change' as a typical short story?
8 Name the main topic of the short story.

9 Examine the narrative perspective used in the short story and explain how this influences the reader's view of the characters (→ Info box, p. 29).

10 Analyse the author's use of language when referring to Laylor.

11 Contrast the situation of the two women.

Feature	Laylor	Narrator
home		
family		
job		
future prospects		

12 Describe the narrator's emotions in the course of the story.

13 **a** Explain the narrator's decision to leave at the end of the story.
b Comment on her decision. Do you think she will regret it?

14 Explain what the symbol of loose change signifies in the short story. Compare your findings to your ideas from **1** (p. 13).

Beyond the text

15 **Speaking** Work in groups of three. One of you is the narrator, one is her good angel (on her right side) and one her bad angel (on her left side). The narrator has to make a decision about helping Laylor, and the two angels are trying to influence her in different directions. Prepare your roles, then sit down next to each other and talk.

16 **Speaking** Work in pairs. Imagine one of you is the narrator and the other is the narrator's grandmother. You meet up for coffee the day after the encounter and the narrator tells her grandmother about meeting Laylor. Prepare some notes, then act out their conversation.

17 You choose:
a **Writing** Write an alternative ending to the story.
OR
b **Writing** Write Laylor's diary entry from the day the two women met.

18 **a** Find one or two pictures to illustrate the cover of a new edition of 'Loose Change'.
b Compare your findings in a group and justify your choice of illustration.

B2 'She Shall Not Be Moved' *Shereen Pandit*

Read the short story and complete the tasks on pp. 28–30.

I swear, if it hadn't been so late, I'd have done something about it. Or if the previous two number 201 buses hadn't vanished into thin air. Or if it hadn't been so cold. Or if I didn't have Mariam with me, her almost turning blue with the cold. Yes, I would definitely have done something about it, there and then. I would have given him a piece of my mind. And them.

But the thing is, it was late, and the buses hadn't come for more than an hour. And this being London, it was pretty darned cold and there was Mariam, shivering next to me. So I was highly pleased, I tell you, when that bus finally pulled up. I paid. That's another thing, it was the last change I had on me and I couldn't afford to get chucked off, could I?

Anyhow, this bus finally comes, I put Mariam up alongside me, while I pay. Then I try to move her along into the bus ahead of me. Only, we can't move. The aisle's blocked by this huge woman, with a pram in the middle of the aisle. She seems to be Somali, from her clothes – long dark dress, hair covered with a veil, like what nuns used to wear, arms covered to the wrists, nothing but face and hands showing. The driver shouts at me to move down the bus, only I can't because of the pram. I'm about to say to him, well get this woman to move out of the way – it's one of those modern buses with a special place for prams – when I see what the problem is.

There are these two women, sitting in those fold up seats in the pram space. White, fifty-ish, wrinkles full of powder and grey roots under the blonde rinse, mouths like dried up prunes, both of them. One of them's wearing a buttoned up cardie like Pauline in *EastEnders*. The other one's wearing a colourless crumpled and none too clean mac of some kind. The bigbreasted, big bottomed type. Both looked strong enough in the arm to lift a good few down the pubs every night.

They're sitting right under that notice which says: 'Please allow wheelchair users and those with prams priority in using this space'. Which means, these two are supposed to get up so the Somali woman can put her pram in the space left when their seats fold up. Only, they're staring hard out of the window, pretending they haven't heard a word of what's going on, and if they did, it's nothing to do with them.

As I said, they didn't look like the kind to tackle unless you wanted a real scene. I wouldn't have put it past the likes of them to use some pretty rough language, regardless of whether there were kids around. Me, I don't like exposing Mariam to unpleasantness. So I turn to the driver, who's still yelling down the aisle from behind his glassed in box. I reckon it's his job to tell the women to move. I mean why should I do his dirty work?

5 give sb. a piece of your mind (infml): tell sb. your opinion
8 pretty darned cold (infml): *verdammt kalt*
11 chuck sb. off (infml): *jdn. hinauswerfen*
14 aisle [aɪl]: Gang
14 pram: carriage for babies
16 veil [veɪl]: *Schleier*
22 fold-up seat: *Klappsitz*
23 fifty-ish: in their fifties
24 rinse [rɪns] (n): artificial colouring
24 prune: *Trockenpflaume*
25 cardie (infml): cardigan
25 *EastEnders*: long-running BBC soap opera
26 mac (infml): mackintosh (raincoat)
28 lift a good few (infml): drink a few pints of beer
35 tackle sb. (infml): *sich mit jdm. anlegen*
36 I wouldn't have put it past them: *ich hätte es ihnen glatt zugetraut*
36 the likes of them (infml): people like them
39 yell (v, infml): shout
40 reckon (infml): suppose
41 dirty work (infml): *Dreckarbeit*

There're two empty seats right opposite the women. They can just move over the aisle. I look hard at them, trying to will them to look around. They finally can't resist looking round to see the havoc they've caused. They're still trying to be nonchalant, but you can see this gleam of satisfaction in their eyes, their mouths growing even thinner as they jam their lips grimly together, as if to say: 'That'll show you who's boss!'.

I take the chance to point the empty seats out to them. Politely. I'm doing as my mum said when I was young, always show them we're better. So, even though I've got a small kid with me, I'm not scrambling to grab the seat. Usually I let Mariam sit down because buses jerking around can be dangerous for kids, especially kids like Mariam, small for her age and skinny to boot. But do these old so-and-so's take the seat I'm pointing out to them? Not likely. They look at me, then look at the seats as if they're a pile of dog dirt I'm offering. Then they mutter something to each other, turn up their noses and stare out the window again, like it's nothing to do with them.

The Somali woman, meantime, has squashed herself tight up against the side of the aisle, just below the stairs. If anyone really wants to, they can squeeze past and go on upstairs. Her face is tight too. Lips set. Eyes blank. Head held high. She looks like a haughty queen. She's done her best to accommodate other passengers by leaving them what inches she can, and now she just shuts off and looks into space.

Through all this, the driver's been yelling on and off. Finally, his door swings open – the glassed-in bit leading into the bus, I mean. Right, I think, here he comes, he's going to make the old witches move. He's not scared of them, big strapping bloke, he doesn't have to be scared of anyone or anything. Besides, he's got right on his side. They can't even complain amongst themselves, let alone to his employers that he's taking sides with the Somali women just because they're both black

But oh no! He comes at this Somali woman and yells at her that either she folds up the pram or she leaves the bus. He's all over her, leaning right into her face and shouting. I reckon he's going to hit her. I hate violence and I turn Mariam's face away. I don't like her seeing ugliness like this. The Somali woman doesn't give an inch. Except to turn aside disdainfully because this bloke's spit is flying in her face. Pulling her wrapper more closely about her, she says scornfully that she's not doing either. And you can see why not. Her baby's asleep in the pram and she's already got another small one hanging onto her. One hand on the pram, another on the toddler.

Her face is full of contempt for this driver, but her voice isn't rude or loud or anything. Just firm. She's paid, she's got these kids, she's staying put. He shouts and storms. Eventually he gives up and goes back and starts the bus so it jerks and she and the kid and the pram nearly go flying, except for the pram being stuck. Me, I'm totally shocked at his attitude. I'm really building up a head of steam here. If it wasn't

43 will sb. to do sth.: make sb. do sth. by wishing for it very strongly
44 havoc [ˈhævək]: chaos
45 nonchalant [ˈnɒnʃələnt]: (French for) relaxed
45 gleam (n): look
50 scramble (v, infml): move quickly
51–52 jerk around (infml): move abruptly
53 skinny (infml): very thin
53 to boot: as well
53 so-and-so (n, infml, derog): person you don't like
55 dog dirt: *Hundedreck, Hundekot*
55 mutter sth.: say sth. quietly
58 squash yourself: press yourself
60 tight: *verschlossen*
61 haughty: *arrogant*
62 accommodate sb.: *jdm. entgegenkommen, Zugeständnisse machen*
67 strapping (infml): big and strong
74 ugliness: (here) an unpleasant incident
76 disdainfully: full of contempt *(Verachtung)*
76 spit (n): *Spucke*
77 scornfully: full of contempt
80 toddler: very young child
86 build up a head of steam (infml): get angry

for all the stuff I said before, at this stage I really would have given him a go. But he's gone back and there's nothing I can do about him.

I tell the Somali woman to sit down in the empty seat, thinking she can at least hold the small one on her lap and maybe I could steady the pram while Mariam sits next to her. She shakes her head wordlessly. It's like she's used up all her words on the driver. I reckon maybe, in spite of her looking so proud and firm, she's too timid to give the women a go. Maybe she's worried, being black and a foreigner, probably a refugee and all. Maybe she also doesn't like a scene and is already embarrassed enough by the women. Maybe if she'd said something to them directly, I would have backed her. But how could I go and attack them out of the blue, make them move, if she's not saying anything to them?

The two women, deciding that they aren't having enough fun, start a loud conversation with each other about how they're not getting up, no way. Cardie reckons to Mac that 'they' – meaning women with prams, or does she mean black women – just pretend 'they' want to park the pram and then snatch the seats. 'They' want everything their way. Definitely black people this time. And on and on they go. I'm fuming, amongst other things, because Mariam is being subjected to all this racist hogwash. But what's the point in having a go? It'll only lead to a row lasting the whole bus ride and I probably will get chucked off then for stirring. Even if I'm in the right. They can say what they like about anti-racist laws, but I've yet to see them stop people like these two slinging their poison around.

I look at the other passengers in the second half of the bus, past the stairs. All white. No-one's saying anything, no-one's seeing anything, no-one's hearing anything. Not their business. Mariam starts to nudge me and whispers to me to tell the driver to tell the old witches to move. She doesn't call them that, though. Calls them 'those two ladies'. Ladies my backside.

Mariam's language is polite, but this is a kid with attitude. Got it from me, I guess. I used to be known as a kid with attitude too. They can have our seats, she says loudly. I nod, but say nothing. Mariam decides to go on, so I feel like really nudging her hard, only I don't hold with hurting kids. They are the problem, she says even more loudly. I look at them again, still saying nothing. I'm still thinking that with the Somali woman saying nothing to them and the driver on their side, I'm going to end up outside in the cold with Mariam, minus the fare, if I take them on.

This is what I'm thinking, but not saying to Mariam. Kids, there are things they just don't understand. I mean, Mariam would definitely not get to her dance lesson on time and then she'd be right miffed. And then there's the busfare and the fees and the time and everything all wasted.

Mariam glares at the women. She glares at me. I know what she's thinking. How many times have I told her to stand up against

87 stage: particular point in time during a process
87–88 give sb. a go: (here) start an argument with sb.
93 timid ['tɪmɪd]: not brave
97–98 out of the blue (infml): without an obvious cause
104 fume (v): be very angry
105 be subjected to sth. [səb'dʒektɪd]: *einer Sache ausgesetzt sein*
106 hogwash (infml): nonsense
107 row [raʊ] (n): quarrel, noisy argument
108 stir (v, infml): cause trouble
110 sling sth. around: throw sth. around in a careless way
113 nudge sb.: *jdn. anstupsen*
115–116 ladies my backside (sl): *von wegen Damen*
118 attitude: firm beliefs
125 take sb. on: *sich mit jdm. anlegen*
128 miffed (infml): upset
130 glare at sb.: look at sb. angrily

wrongdoing. How many times have I pushed her into standing up against bullies at school, whether they're bullying her or someone else. And her only such a small kid for her age.

We try to bring her up thinking about right and wrong. Like how many times have I told her that I'm only living in this miserable country because I'd got into trouble back home, fighting for our rights. There are political posters and slogans all over the house. One of them's got Pastor Neumuller's speech: 'First they came for the Jews …' and all that. She knows, all right. She knows that I should be speaking up for this Somali woman.

And here I'm saying nothing, doing nothing. Every once in a while, when people get on and mutter about the aisle being blocked, the driver shouts at the Somali woman. She stands there like a rock. Cardie and Mac have restarted their loud conversation about 'them' wanting to take everything over. I laugh in their faces and start agreeing loudly with Mariam, but I don't say anything to them. The bus is filling up. At a couple of stops some pretty yobbo looking types get on. You know, tattoos, earrings all over their faces, hair sticking up. The type that I can't afford to get tangled with. I don't fancy a boot in my face. Or in Mariam's. While those two probably watch and cheer. The yobbos just squeeze past the Somali woman. It's a couple of blokes in collars and ties that swear at her before they force a path upstairs, nearly making her let go of the pram and fall. You can't always tell by appearances can you.

Then the bus empties a bit. Another middle-aged woman gets on, about the same age as the two troublemakers. But this one's sort of frailer looking. Now my mum, when we were kids, she'd only have given us what-for if we didn't get up and offer our seats to older people. I've still got the habit drilled into me. I don't like Mariam getting up, like I said, in case she falls, so usually I give up my seat. But this time, I sit tight. Mariam gives me a questioning look, then makes to get up for this new old lady, but I pull her down. Call me a reverse racist if you like, but if those white women won't get up for the Somali woman, then I'm not giving my seat or my kid's to one of their kind. No way. I didn't start this.

Now they start a loud conversation about the 'their' manners. Meaning me. I glare at them and say nothing. I can feel Mariam wriggling with impatience for me to mouth off at them. But I reckon with the driver on their side, even against this poor woman with her pram and her kids, what chance have I got? He'd probably call the police for me, if I gave them lip. And guess whose side the police would be on! So I glare and sit tight. I stare straight ahead, like this old lady standing is nothing to do with me. I can feel my lips tighten with satisfaction at getting back at the other two. See how they feel when it's one of their kind getting a dose of it.

132 wrongdoing (n): *Unrecht*
139 Pastor Neumuller: Martin Niemöller, German Protestant pastor who criticized himself publicly for failing to defend the victims of Hitler's regime
148 yobbo (sl): loud, aggressive person
150 get tangled with sb. (infml): get involved with sb.
150 fancy sth.: want to have sth.
158 frail: *zerbrechlich*
158–159 give sb. what-for (infml): criticize or punish sb. for bad behaviour
169 wriggle: *zucken*
169 mouth off at sb. (infml): tell sb. what you think in a very direct way
172 give sb. lip (infml): speak to sb. in a rude way
175 get back at sb. (infml): *jdm. etwas heimzahlen*

But I'm feeling right small inside. I feel like a real sod. Not only for not standing up for the Somali woman, but for not giving my seat to the old white woman. Plus Mariam starts hassling about getting up for the old woman. I almost blow my top at Mariam. I mean, can't she see what I'm doing? Standing up to them? I pull her down again and glare at her, whispering 'No!' fiercely at her as she struggles to stand up and give her seat to the old woman standing.

Then I feel like a right idiot, getting upset at Mariam. The kid's only doing what she's been taught. I make my excuses to Mariam, but she's not taking any notice of me. She doesn't exactly look like she wants to cry, like when she's mad at me, though. Her face is just the same as usual, not swelling up and going red like it always does before she starts to cry, but her eyes have that sad, lost, grief-stricken look. I sit there feeling right helpless. I'm trying to remember where I know that look from.

The bus is coming to a main shopping area, people are walking around with holly-printed plastic bags full of goodies. That makes me remember when Mariam had that look on her face. She had it when she woke up in the night last Christmas and found her Dad stuffing her stocking. I feel sick at the thought of what she's thinking of me. The thing is, what can I do? You can teach kids to stand up against bullies, but sometimes they've got to learn discretion is the better part of valour. I start to explain, but Mariam isn't taking any notice. She looks again at the old woman swaying about on the bus, trying to hold on to prevent herself falling. Then she gives me a look – like I've chucked away her favourite teddy bear.

At last we get to Woodgreen and the troublemakers get off, slinging a last few barbs over their shoulders. At that, the Somali woman finally snaps. She lets go of the pram and leans out the doorway and shouts 'racists!' after them. They're still hurling abuse at her, as if they were the injured parties, as they disappear into the crowd, everybody staring. But thank god, it's Woodgreen and the sea of faces staring interestedly at us is as much black as white.

The Somali woman starts to struggle to turn the pram so she can get off too. I offer to help her, muttering to her that she should report the driver. What's the good of that, she says bitterly. But why do you think he's taking their part, I ask her, because I am truly confused. I mean he's a black man. The black woman is clearly in the right, so, as I said before, he can't get into trouble with the company if he tells the white women to get up or get off.

The Somali woman gives me a long look: 'Because he's a slave,' she says. 'He is a slave,' she repeats loudly through the still open back door of the bus, at the driver collecting fares from passengers boarding at the front. I realise from her attitude that they probably already played it all out, she and the women and the driver, before I got on the bus.

177 sod (sl): nasty person
179 hassle (v, infml): complain, make trouble
180 blow your top at sb. (infml): get very angry with sb.
182 fierce: very angry
189 grief-stricken: full of sorrow
193 holly: *Stechpalme (typischer Weihnachtsschmuck)*
195 stuffing her stocking: British Christmas custom
198 discretion [dɪˈskreʃn] is the better part of valour [ˈvælə]: quotation based on Shakespeare, Henry IV, Part 1 *(Klugheit ist der bessere Teil der Tapferkeit)*
205 snap (v): lose control
206 hurl abuse [əˈbjuːs] at sb.: shout insults at sb.
211 report sb.: make a formal complaint about sb.

'But me,' she says, looking at me hard again, 'I am not a slave. I would rather die than be one.' Her voice is like granite, hard and unmovable. Every word falls heavy as a stone between us, cuts into me like a diamond.

I feel my face turn red as I take Mariam's hand. All through Mariam's class, that woman's words go round and round in my head. I reckon it's me she's called a slave too, for not sticking up for her. And the thing is, I'm not even mad at her if that's what she's saying. I'm just upset at myself for not doing anything.

And then there's Mariam. People reckon kids forget things quickly. But I know Mariam. All afternoon I sit there watching her. I want to tell her she still shouldn't let people walk all over her, just because they're white, or stronger, or richer, or anything. I don't want her not to stick up for other people if she sees wrong done to them. But I also want to tell her that you can't always do that – you've got to pick your moments. Then I ask myself what's the good of raking it all up again? What's done is done.

After her class, Mariam asks to go to the bagel shop for a hot buttered bagel. This is our usual routine, our little treat. I suggest an extra special treat instead. I take Mariam for a pizza and let her have Coke as extra, extra special. She looks puzzled for a moment at all this, but then she's yakking away, back to her usual bouncy self. I reckon there's nothing like a special treat to let kids forget bad memories. Soon she's blowing bubbles into her Coke through her straw. She's got a smear of pizza tomato on her cheek.

So why can't I forget the whole thing? Is it because I imagine a bit of Mariam's look of this afternoon still about her every time she looks at me?

From: Maggie Hamand (publisher): Underwords: The Hidden City. *London: Maia Press, 2005, pp. 35–46*

237 rake sth. up (infml): begin talking about sth. unpleasant again
243 yak (v, infml): talk continuously about nothing important
243 bouncy (infml): lively, happy

Info Shereen Pandit

Shereen Pandit is originally from South Africa. After studying law and becoming a lawyer and political activist, she came in conflict with the South African government. For this reason, she was forced to flee to the UK in 1987. As she wasn't allowed to practise law in the UK, she turned to writing for a living. In addition to her journalistic work, she has written a number of short stories that have appeared in many anthologies and magazines and have won several prizes.

Comprehension

1 Summarize the plot of the story in no more than four sentences.

2 Read the following statements about the narrator of the story and mark them as true of false. Support your answer by adding a line number and quote from the text.

Statements	True	False
A The narrator is a woman. line(s): ____________ quote: ____		
B The narrator is a person of colour. line(s): ____________ quote: ____		
C The narrator is a political refugee. line(s): ____________ quote: ____		
D The narrator has just arrived in the UK. line(s): ____________ quote: ____		
E The narrator has a well-paid job. line(s): ____________ quote: ____		
F The narrator loves the UK. line(s): ____________ quote: ____		

Analysis

3 a Compare the following text with the opening paragraphs of the story (ll. 1–11):

It was cold, even by London standards, and she had been waiting over an hour for the bus to come. And then there was Mariam, almost blue with cold, shivering at her side. So when the number 201 bus finally wheeled into sight, her heart surged with relief. She rummaged in her purse for the fare. Just barely enough for the two of them. She certainly didn't want to risk getting chucked off the bus this time, did she?

b Analyse how the two texts differ in their effect on the reader. Pay special attention to the point of view.

Info Point of view

The narrator of a story can be a character of the story, or a nameless voice that tells the story without taking part in it. A **first-person narrator** refers to him- or herself as 'I' and tells the story from their own personal point of view. First-person narration is always connected with a **limited point of view** because one character cannot possibly know everything that is happening.
Alternatively, a story can be told in the **third person**. In this case, the narrator is a nameless voice that doesn't belong to the plot. The narrator may, however, have a **limited point of view**, i. e. the narrator only knows and sees what one particular character knows and sees (single-character point of view). In a longer text (e. g. a novel), the narrative perspective may jump from one character to another (multiple-character point of view). In traditional novels, the narrator is often an independent voice that stands above the action of the plot and thus has an **unlimited point of view**.

4 a With a partner, analyse the narrator's strategy by making two lists: One of you collects reasons why the narrator feels that (s)he should intervene, the other collects reasons why the narrator shouldn't intervene.

b Compare your findings and draw conclusions.

Beyond the text

5 Assess the narrator's behaviour. Do you think (s)he makes the right decision?

6 **Writing** Taking the narrator's point of view, write a letter of complaint to London Transport to report the incident on the bus. Explain why you are dissatisfied with the driver's behavior.

Language help

racist: *Rassist/in; rassistisch* · prejudice · (un)prejudiced · bias · (un)biased · allusion (to) · allude (to)

7 a **Listening** You are going to hear an excerpt from a podcast in which two British Asian journalists discuss racism in the UK. You will hear the excerpt twice. While listening, mark the statements below as true or false.

	True	False
A Both speakers say that when they were children, they were ashamed of their non-English identity.		
B A new survey has revealed that racism has almost disappeared from British society.		
C One of the women says that ideas of beauty shown in the media are racially biased.		
D Afua says that she didn't learn the term 'unconscious bias' until she was in her twenties.		
E People who have an unconscious bias know that they are being racist.		
F More than twice as many members of ethnic minorities in the UK feel that they have been treated unfairly compared to white people.		
G Members of ethnic minorities complain about being regarded as shoplifters when they enter a shop.		
H Racist violence is still a problem in Britain.		

b Discuss how (implicit or open) racism influences the way the characters behave in 'She Shall Not Be Moved'.

B3 'The Third and Final Continent' *Jhumpa Lahiri*

Read the short story and complete the tasks on pp. 45–47.

I left India in 1964 with a certificate in commerce and the equivalent, in those days, of ten dollars to my name. For three weeks I sailed on the S. S. Roma, an Italian cargo vessel, in a cabin next to the ship's engine, across the Arabian Sea, the Red Sea, the Mediterranean, and finally to England. I lived in London, in Finsbury Park, in a house occupied entirely by penniless Bengali bachelors like myself, at least a dozen and sometimes more, all struggling to educate and establish ourselves abroad.

I attended lectures at L. S. E. and worked at the university library to get by. We lived three or four to a room, shared a single, icy toilet, and took turns cooking pots of egg curry, which we ate with our hands on a table covered with newspapers. Apart from our jobs we had few responsibilities. On weekends we lounged barefoot in drawstring

3 cargo vessel: *Frachtschiff*
9 L. S. E. = London School of Economics and Political Science: prestigious university in London
13 lounge (v): relax
13 drawstring: string through the top of a piece of clothing that can be pulled tighter

pajamas, drinking tea and smoking Rothmans, or set out to watch cricket at Lord's. Some weekends the house was crammed with still more Bengalis, to whom we had introduced ourselves at the greengrocer, or on the Tube, and we made yet more egg curry, and played Mukesh on a Grundig reel-to-reel, and soaked our dirty dishes in the bathtub. Every now and then someone in the house moved out, to live with a woman whom his family back in Calcutta had determined he was to wed. In 1969, when I was thirty-six years old, my own marriage was arranged. Around the same time, I was offered a full-time job in America, in the processing department of a library at M. I. T. The salary was generous enough to support a wife, and I was honored to be hired by a world-famous university, and so I obtained a green card, and prepared to travel farther still.

By then I had enough money to go by plane. I flew first to Calcutta, to attend my wedding, and a week later to Boston, to begin my new job. During the flight I read 'The Student Guide to North America,' for although I was no longer a student, I was on a budget all the same. I learned that Americans drove on the right side of the road, not the left, and that they called a lift an elevator and an engaged phone busy. 'The pace of life in North America is different from Britain, as you will soon discover,' the guidebook informed me. 'Everybody feels he must get to the top. Don't expect an English cup of tea.' As the plane began its descent over Boston Harbor, the pilot announced the weather and the time, and that President Nixon had declared a national holiday: two American men had landed on the moon. Several passengers cheered. 'God bless America!' one of them hollered. Across the aisle, I saw a woman praying.

I spent my first night at the Y. M. C. A. in Central Square, Cambridge, an inexpensive accommodation recommended by my guidebook which was within walking distance of M. I. T. The room contained a cot, a desk, and a small wooden cross on one wall. A sign on the door said that cooking was strictly forbidden. A bare window overlooked Massachusetts Avenue. Car horns, shrill and prolonged, blared one after another. Sirens and flashing lights heralded endless emergencies, and a succession of buses rumbled past, their doors opening and closing with a powerful hiss, throughout the night. The noise was constantly distracting, at times suffocating. I felt it deep in my ribs, just as I had felt the furious drone of the engine on the S. S. Roma. But there was no ship's deck to escape to, no glittering ocean to thrill my soul, no breeze to cool my face, no one to talk to. I was too tired to pace the gloomy corridors of the Y. M. C. A. in my pajamas. Instead I sat at the desk and stared out the window. In the morning I reported to my job at the Dewey Library, a beige fortlike building by Memorial Drive. I also opened a bank account, rented a post-office box, and bought a plastic bowl and a spoon. I went to a supermarket called Purity Supreme, wandering up

15 Lord's = Lord's Cricket Ground: popular cricket venue in Westminster
17 Mukesh = Mukesh Chand Mathor (1923–1976): Indian singer
18 Grundig reel-to-reel: German tape recorder *(Spulentonbandgerät)*
18 soak sth.: put sth. into a liquid to wash it
20 determine sth. [dɪˈtɜːmɪn]: *etwas bestimmen*
20 wed sb.: marry sb.
23 M. I. T. = Massachusetts Institute of Technology: US university
25 green card: card that allows non-Americans to live and work in the USA
30 be on a budget [ˈbʌdʒɪt]: *auf sein Geld achten müssen*
33 pace (n): speed at which sth. happens
36 descent [dɪˈsent]: *Landeanflug*
39 holler (infml): shout loudly
39 aisle [aɪl]: *Gang (zwischen Sitzreihen)*
41 Y. M. C. A. = Young Men's Christian Association: organization that offers sports facilities and hostels for young people
43 cot: simple bed
46 blare (v): make a loud noise
47 herald sth. [ˈherəld]: announce sth.
50 distracting: annoying
50 suffocating [ˈsʌfəkeɪtɪŋ]: making it impossible to breathe
51 drone (n): loud, deep noise
53–54 pace the corridors: walk up and down the corridors
53 gloomy: dark and depressing
56 fortlike: like a fort

and down the aisles, comparing prices with those in England. In the end I bought a carton of milk and a box of cornflakes. This was my first meal in America. Even the simple chore of buying milk was new to me; in London we'd had bottles delivered each morning to our door.

In a week I had adjusted, more or less. I ate cornflakes and milk morning and night, and bought some bananas for variety, slicing them into the bowl with the edge of my spoon. I left my carton of milk on the shaded part of the windowsill, as I had seen other residents at the Y. M. C. A. do. To pass the time in the evenings I read the *Boston Globe* downstairs, in a spacious room with stained-glass windows. I read every article and advertisement, so that I would grow familiar with things, and when my eyes grew tired I slept. Only I did not sleep well. Each night I had to keep the window wide open; it was the only source of air in the stifling room, and the noise was intolerable. I would lie on the cot with my fingers pressed into my ears, but when I drifted off to sleep my hands fell away, and the noise of the traffic would wake me up again. Pigeon feathers drifted onto the windowsill, and one evening, when I poured milk over my cornflakes, I saw that it had soured. Nevertheless I resolved to stay at the Y. M. C. A. for six weeks, until my wife's passport and green card were ready. Once she arrived I would have to rent a proper apartment, and from time to time I studied the classified section of the newspaper, or stopped in at the housing office at M. I. T. during my lunch break to see what was available. It was in this manner that I discovered a room for immediate occupancy, in a house on a quiet street, the listing said, for eight dollars per week. I dialled the number from a pay telephone, sorting through the coins, with which I was still unfamiliar, smaller and lighter than shillings, heavier and brighter than paisas.

'Who is speaking?' a woman demanded. Her voice was bold and clamorous.

'Yes, good afternoon, Madam. I am calling about the room for rent.'

'Harvard or Tech?'

'I beg your pardon?'

'Are you from Harvard or Tech?'

Gathering that Tech referred to the Massachusetts Institute of Technology, I replied, 'I work at Dewey Library,' adding tentatively, 'at Tech.'

'I only rent rooms to boys from Harvard or Tech!'

'Yes, Madam.'

I was given an address and an appointment for seven o'clock that evening. Thirty minutes before the hour I set out, my guidebook in my pocket, my breath fresh with Listerine. I turned down a street shaded with trees, perpendicular to Massachusetts Avenue. In spite of the heat I wore a coat and tie, regarding the event as I would any other interview; I had never lived in the home of a person who was not Indian. The house,

61 chore [tʃɔː]: task
63 adjust [əˈdʒʌst]: *sich anpassen*
67 Boston Globe: Boston newspaper
68 spacious [ˈspeɪʃəs]: large
68 stained-glass windows: coloured windows like in a church
72 stifling [ˈstaɪflɪŋ]: hot
75 pigeon [ˈpɪdʒɪn]: *Taube*
75 windowsill: *Fensterbank, Fensterbrett*
77 resolve to do [rɪˈzɒlv]: firmly decide to do
78 rent sth.: *etwas mieten*
79 classified section: part in a newspaper that contains private adverts
82 occupancy [ˈɒkjəpənsi] (fml): *Bewohnen, Bezug*
83 listing: *Eintrag; (hier) Anzeige*
86 paisa [ˈpaɪsɑː, ˈpaɪsə]: a small Indian coin
88 clamorous [ˈklæmərəs] (fml): *laut, forsch*
91 I beg your pardon (fml): phrase used to ask sb. to repeat sth. because you did not hear them
93 gather (that) …: conclude, believe (that) …
94 tentative [ˈtentətɪv]: cautious
100 Listerine [ˈlɪstəriːn]: a brand of mouthwash
101 perpendicular [ˌpɜːpənˈdɪkjələ]: at a 90° angle

surrounded by a chain-link fence, was off-white with dark-brown trim, with a tangle of forsythia bushes plastered against its front and sides. When I pressed the bell, the woman with whom I had spoken on the phone hollered from what seemed to be just the other side of the door, 'One minute, please!'

Several minutes later the door was opened by a tiny, extremely old woman. A mass of snowy hair was arranged like a small sack on top of her head. As I stepped into the house she sat down on a wooden bench positioned at the bottom of a narrow carpeted staircase. Once she was settled on the bench, in a small pool of light, she peered up at me, giving me her undivided attention. She wore a long black skirt that spread like a stiff tent to the floor, and a starched white shirt edged with ruffles at the throat and cuffs. Her hands, folded together in her lap, had long pallid fingers, with swollen knuckles and tough yellow nails. Age had battered her features so that she almost resembled a man, with sharp, shrunken eyes and prominent creases on either side of her nose. Her lips, chapped and faded, had nearly disappeared, and her eyebrows were missing altogether. Nevertheless she looked fierce.

'Lock up!' she commanded. She shouted even though I stood only a few feet away. 'Fasten the chain and firmly press that button on the knob! This is the first thing you shall do when you enter, is that clear?'

I locked the door as directed and examined the house. Next to the bench was a small round table, its legs fully concealed, much like the woman's, by a skirt of lace. The table held a lamp, a transistor radio, a leather change purse with a silver clasp, and a telephone. A thick wooden cane was propped against one side. There was a parlor to my right, lined with bookcases and filled with shabby claw-footed furniture. In the corner of the parlor I saw a grand piano with its top down, piled with papers. The piano's bench was missing; it seemed to be the one on which the woman was sitting. Somewhere in the house a clock chimed seven times.

'You're punctual!' the woman proclaimed. 'I expect you shall be so with the rent!'

'I have a letter, Madam.' In my jacket pocket was a letter from M. I. T. confirming my employment, which I had brought along to prove that I was indeed from Tech.

She stared at the letter, then handed it back to me carefully, gripping it with her fingers as if it were a plate heaped with food. She did not wear glasses, and I wondered if she'd read a word of it. 'The last boy was always late! Still owes me eight dollars! Harvard boys aren't what they used to be! Only Harvard and Tech in this house! How's Tech, boy?'

'It is very well.'

'You checked the lock?'

'Yes, Madam.'

104 chain-link fence: *Maschendrahtzaun*
104 off-white (adj): slightly tinted shade of white
105 tangle: *Gestrüpp*
112 carpeted: covered with carpeting *(Teppichboden)*
113 peer (v): look closely
115 ruffles (pl): *Rüschen*
116 cuff: *Manschette*
117 pallid [ˈpælɪd]: pale, without colour
118 batter sth.: beat or attack sth.
118 features (pl): *Gesichtszüge*
119 shrunken: *geschrumpft; (hier) tiefliegend*
119 prominent [ˈprɒmɪnənt]: easily noticed
119 crease [kriːs] (n): fold in sb.'s skin, wrinkle
120 chapped: *rissig*
121 fierce: tough
126 conceal sth. [kənˈsiːl] (fml): hide sth. from view
127 lace: *Spitze (textile Verzierung)*
128 change purse: *Geldbeutel für Kleingeld*
128 clasp: *Verschluss*
129 cane: *Spazierstock*
129 prop sth. against sth.: *etwas an etwas (an)lehnen*
129 parlor (old-fashioned): living room
131 grand piano: *Konzertflügel*
133 chime [tʃaɪm] (v): ring to show the time
135 punctual [ˈpʌŋktʃuəl]: on time
141 heaped with sth.: *mit etwas vollgepackt*
143 owe sb. sth. [əʊ]: *jdm. etw. schulden*

She unclasped her fingers, slapped the space beside her on the bench with one hand, and told me to sit down. For a moment she was silent. Then she intoned, as if she alone possessed this knowledge:

'There is an American flag on the moon!'

'Yes, Madam.' Until then I had not thought very much about the moon shot. It was in the newspaper, of course, article upon article. The astronauts had landed on the shores of the Sea of Tranquility, I had read, travelling farther than anyone in the history of civilization. For a few hours they explored the moon's surface. They gathered rocks in their pockets, described their surroundings (a magnificent desolation, according to one astronaut), spoke by phone to the President, and planted a flag in lunar soil. The voyage was hailed as man's most awesome achievement.

The woman bellowed, 'A flag on the moon, boy! I heard it on the radio! Isn't that splendid?'

'Yes, Madam.'

But she was not satisfied with my reply. Instead she commanded, 'Say 'Splendid!''

I was both baffled and somewhat insulted by the request. It reminded me of the way I was taught multiplication tables as a child, repeating after the master, sitting cross-legged on the floor of my one-room Tollygunge school. It also reminded me of my wedding, when I had repeated endless Sanskrit verses after the priest, verses I barely understood, which joined me to my wife. I said nothing.

'Say 'Splendid!'' the woman bellowed once again.

'Splendid,' I murmured. I had to repeat the word a second time at the top of my lungs, so she could hear. I was reluctant to raise my voice to an elderly woman, but she did not appear to be offended. If anything the reply pleased her, because her next command was:

'Go see the room!'

I rose from the bench and mounted the narrow staircase. There were five doors, two on either side of an equally narrow hallway, and one at the opposite end. Only one door was open. The room contained a twin bed under a sloping ceiling, a brown oval rug, a basin with an exposed pipe, and a chest of drawers. One door led to a closet, another to a toilet and a tub. The window was open; net curtains stirred in the breeze. I lifted them away and inspected the view: a small back yard, with a few fruit trees and an empty clothesline. I was satisfied.

When I returned to the foyer the woman picked up the leather change purse on the table, opened the clasp, fished about with her fingers, and produced a key on a thin wire hoop. She informed me that there was a kitchen at the back of the house, accessible through the parlor. I was welcome to use the stove as long as I left it as I found it. Sheets and towels were provided, but keeping them clean was my own responsibility. The rent was due Friday mornings on the ledge above the piano keys.

148 unclasp sth.: *etwas aufmachen, öffnen*
148 slap sth.: hit sth. with a flat hand
150 intone sth. (fml): say sth. slowly and clearly
153 moon shot: first manned flight to the moon (July 1969)
157 magnificent [mæg'nɪfɪsnt]: very good
157 desolation [ˌdesə'leɪʃn]: *Trostlosigkeit, Verlassenheit*
158 according to sb.: *laut Aussage von jdm.*
159 hail sth. as sth.: praise sth. as sth.
160 achievement: *Leistung*
161 bellow (v): shout
162 splendid: great
166 baffle sb.: confuse sb.
168 cross-legged: *im Schneidersitz*
169 Tollygunge: place in South Kolkota
170 Sanskrit ['sænskrɪt]: ancient language of India
173 murmur ['mɜːmə]: say in a soft voice
173–174 at the top of my lungs: as loud as I could
174 reluctant [rɪ'lʌktənt]: unwilling
175 offend sb. [ə'fend]: *jdn. beleidigen*
178 mount sth. (fml): climb sth.
181 sloping: *schräg*
181 basin ['beɪsn]: *Waschbecken*
182 chest of drawers [drɔːz]: *Kommode*
182 closet ['klɒzɪt]: small room in which clothes are kept
183 tub: *Badewanne*
183 stir: move gently
188 hoop: piece of wire, etc. bent to form a circle
189 accessible [ək'sesəbl]: *zugänglich*
190 stove: *Herd*
190 sheet: *Bettlaken*
192 due: *fällig*
192 ledge: *Brett, Ablage*
192 piano keys: *Tasten*

'And no lady visitors!'

'I am a married man, Madam.' It was the first time I had announced this fact to anyone.

But she had not heard. 'No lady visitors!' she insisted. She introduced herself as Mrs. Croft.

My wife's name was Mala. The marriage had been arranged by my older brother and his wife. I regarded the proposition with neither objection nor enthusiasm. It was a duty expected of me, as it was expected of every man. She was the daughter of a schoolteacher in Beleghata. I was told that she could cook, knit, embroider, sketch landscapes, and recite poems by Tagore, but these talents could not make up for the fact that she did not possess a fair complexion, and so a string of men had rejected her to her face. She was twenty-seven, an age when her parents had begun to fear that she would never marry, and so they were willing to ship their only child halfway across the world in order to save her from spinsterhood.

For five nights we shared a bed. Each of those nights, after applying cold cream and braiding her hair, she turned from me and wept; she missed her parents. Although I would be leaving the country in a few days, custom dictated that she was now a part of my household, and for the next six weeks she was to live with my brother and his wife, cooking, cleaning, serving tea and sweets to guests. I did nothing to console her. I lay on my own side of the bed, reading my guidebook by flashlight. At times I thought of the tiny roo on the other side of the wall which had belonged to my mother. Now the room was practically empty; the wooden pallet on which she'd once slept was piled with trunks and old bedding. Nearly six years ago, before leaving for London, I had watched her die on that bed, had found her playing with her excrement in her final days. Before we cremated her I had cleaned each of her fingernails with a hairpin, and then, because my brother could not bear it, I had assumed the role of eldest son, and had touched the flame to her temple, to release her tormented soul to heaven.

The next morning I moved into Mrs. Croft's house. When I unlocked the door I saw that she was sitting on the piano bench, on the same side as the previous evening. She wore the same black skirt, the same starched white blouse, and had her hands folded together the same way in her lap. She looked so much the same that I wondered if she'd spent the whole night on the bench. I put my suitcase upstairs and then headed off to work. That evening when I came home from the university, she was still there.

'Sit down, boy!' She slapped the space beside her.

I perched on the bench. I had a bag of groceries with me – more milk, more cornflakes, and more bananas, for my inspection of the kitchen earlier in the day had revealed no spare pots or pans. There were only

196 insist: *beharren, bekräftigen*
199 proposition [ˌprɒpəˈzɪʃn]: suggestion
200 objection: *Ablehnung*
202 Beleghata: district of Kolkata (India)
202 knit: *stricken*
202 embroider: *sticken*
203 Tagore = Rabindranath Tagore (1861–1941): Indian poet, artist and musician; first non-European to win the Nobel Prize in Literature (1913).
204 complexion: *Teint*
205 string (of): *Reihe (von)*
205 reject sb. [rɪˈdʒekt]: *jdn. ablehnen*
208 spinsterhood: living unmarried (as a woman)
209 apply sth.: *etwas anwenden*
210 cold cream: *Gesichts-, Feuchtigkeitscreme*
210 braid sth.: *etwas flechten*
210 wept: simple past of weep (cry)
212 custom: *Brauch, Sitte*
215 console sb. [kənˈsəʊl]: *jdn. trösten*
216 flashlight: small electric lamp
218 pallet [ˈpælət]: simple bed filled with straw
218 piled with sth.: *mit etwas beladen*
223 assume a role (fml): *eine Rolle übernehmen*
223 the role of the eldest son: among Hindus the eldest son usually performs the cremation ceremony
224 temple: *Schläfe*
224 release sb.: *jdn. freilassen*
224 tormented [tɔːˈmentɪd]: *gequält*
227 previous [ˈpriːviəs]: coming before
234 perch on sth. (infml): sit on sth.
234 groceries (pl): food and other products sold at a supermarket

two saucepans in the refrigerator, both containing some orange broth, and a copper kettle on the stove.

'Good evening, Madam.'

She asked me if I had checked the lock. I told her I had.

For a moment she was silent. Then suddenly she declared, with the equal measures of disbelief and delight as the night before, 'There's an American flag on the moon, boy!'

'Yes, Madam.'

'A flag on the moon! Isn't that splendid?'

I nodded, dreading what I knew was coming. 'Yes, Madam.'

'Say 'Splendid!''

This time I paused, looking to either side in case anyone was there to overhear me, though I knew perfectly well that the house was empty. I felt like an idiot. But it was a small enough thing to ask. 'Splendid!' I cried out.

Within days it became our routine. In the mornings when I left for the library Mrs. Croft was either hidden away in her bedroom, on the other side of the staircase, or sitting on the bench, oblivious of my presence, listening to the news or classical music on the radio. But each evening when I returned the same thing happened: she slapped the bench, ordered me to sit down, declared that there was a flag on the moon, and declared that it was splendid. I said it was splendid, too, and then we sat in silence. As awkward as it was, and as endless as it felt to me then, the nightly encounter lasted only about ten minutes; inevitably she would drift off to sleep, her head falling abruptly toward her chest, leaving me free to retire to my room. By then, of course, there was no flag standing on the moon. The astronauts, I read in the paper, had seen it fall before they flew back to Earth. But I did not have the heart to tell her.

Friday morning, when my first week's rent was due, I went to the piano in the parlor to place my money on the ledge. The piano keys were dull and discolored. When I pressed one, it made no sound at all. I had put eight dollar bills in an envelope and written Mrs. Croft's name on the front of it. I was not in the habit of leaving money unmarked and unattended. From where I stood I could see the profile of her tent-shaped skirt in the hall. It seemed unnecessary to make her get up and walk all the way to the piano. I never saw her walking about, and assumed, from the cane propped against the round table, that she did so with difficulty. When I approached the bench she peered up at me and demanded:

'What is your business?'

'The rent, Madam.'

'On the ledge above the piano keys!'

'I have it here.' I extended the envelope toward her, but her fingers, folded together in her lap, did not budge. I bowed slightly and lowered

237 saucepan [ˈsɔːspən]: metal pot
237 broth [brɒθ]: *Brühe*
242 measure [ˈmeʒə]: *Maß, Ausmaß*
242 delight: pleasure
246 nod: *nicken*
246 dread sth. [dred]: greatly fear sth.
254 be oblivious of sth. [əˈblɪviəs]: not be aware of sth.
260 encounter (n): *Begegnung*
260 inevitably [ɪnˈevɪtəbli]: without exception
268 dull: *stumpf*
281 budge: move

the envelope, so that it hovered just above her hands. After a moment she accepted it, and nodded her head. That night when I came home, she did not slap the bench, but out of habit I sat beside her as usual. She asked me if I had checked the lock, but she mentioned nothing about the flag on the moon. Instead she said:

'It was very kind of you!'

'I beg your pardon, Madam?'

'Very kind of you!'

She was still holding the envelope in her hands.

On Sunday there was a knock on my door. An elderly woman introduced herself: she was Mrs. Croft's daughter, Helen. She walked into the room and looked at each of the walls as if for signs of change, glancing at the shirts that hung in the closet, the neckties draped over the doorknob, the box of cornflakes on the chest of drawers, the dirty bowl and spoon in the basin. She was short and thickwaisted, with cropped silver hair and bright pink lipstick. She wore a sleeveless summer dress, a necklace of white plastic beads, and spectacles on a chain that hung like a swing against her chest. The backs of her legs were mapped with dark-blue veins, and her upper arms sagged like the flesh of a roasted eggplant. She told me she lived in Arlington, a town farther up Massachusetts Avenue. 'I come once a week to bring Mother groceries. Has she sent you packing yet?'

'It is very well, Madam.'

'Some of the boys run screaming. But I think she likes you. You're the first boarder she's ever referred to as a gentleman.'

She looked at me, noticing my bare feet. (I still felt strange wearing shoes indoors, and always removed them before entering my room.) 'Are you new to Boston?'

'New to America, Madam.'

'From?' She raised her eyebrows.

'I am from Calcutta, India.'

'Is that right? We had a Brazilian fellow, about a year ago. You'll find Cambridge a very international city.'

I nodded, and began to wonder how long our conversation would last. But at that moment we heard Mrs. Croft's electrifying voice rising up the stairs.

'You are to come downstairs immediately!'

'What is it?' Helen cried back.

'Immediately!'

I put on my shoes. Helen sighed.

I followed Helen down the staircase. She seemed to be in no hurry, and complained at one point that she had a bad knee. 'Have you been walking without your cane?' Helen called out. 'You know you're not supposed to walk without that cane.' She paused, resting her hand on the bannister, and looked back at me. 'She slips sometimes.'

282 hover [ˈhɒvə]: *(in der Luft) schweben*
294 glance (v): look briefly
294 necktie: *Krawatte, Schlips*
296 thickwaisted: *dick um die Taille*
297 cropped: cut short
297 sleeveless: *ärmellos*
298 necklace [ˈnekləs]: *Halskette*
298 spectacles [ˈspektəktəlz] (pl, old-fashioned): eyeglasses
299 swing: *Schaukel*
300 mapped: marked
300 sag: *durchhängen*
301 eggplant: *Aubergine*
303 groceries (pl): food and other things bought at a supermarket
303 send sb. packing (infml): send sb. away
306 boarder: *Untermieter/in*
316 electrifying: attracting attention
326 bannister [ˈbænɪstə]: handrail
326 slip (v): *ausrutschen*

For the first time Mrs. Croft seemed vulnerable. I pictured her on the floor in front of the bench, flat on her back, staring at the ceiling, her feet pointing in opposite directions. But when we reached the bottom of the staircase she was sitting there as usual, her hands folded together in her lap. Two grocery bags were at her feet. She did not slap the bench, or ask us to sit down. She glared.

'What is it, Mother?'

'It's improper!'

'What's improper?'

'It is improper for a lady and gentleman who are not married to one another to hold a private conversation without a chaperone!'

Helen said she was sixty-eight years old, old enough to be my mother, but Mrs. Croft insisted that Helen and I speak to each other downstairs, in the parlor. She added that it was also improper for a lady of Helen's station to reveal her age, and to wear a dress so high above the ankle.

'For your information, Mother, it's 1969. What would you do if you actually left the house one day and saw a girl in a miniskirt?'

Mrs. Croft sniffed. 'I'd have her arrested.'

Helen shook her head and picked up one of the grocery bags. I picked up the other one, and followed her through the parlor and into the kitchen. The bags were filled with cans of soup, which Helen opened up one by one with a few cranks of a can opener. She tossed the old soup into the sink, rinsed the saucepans under the tap, filled them with soup from the newly opened cans, and put them back in the refrigerator. A few years ago she could still open the cans herself,' Helen said. 'She hates that I do it for her now. But the piano killed her hands.' She put on her spectacles, glanced at the cupboards, and spotted my tea bags. 'Shall we have a cup?'

I filled the kettle on the stove. 'I beg your pardon, Madam. The piano?'

'She used to give lessons. For forty years. It was how she raised us after my father died.' Helen put her hands on her hips, staring at the open refrigerator. She reached into the back, pulled out a wrapped stick of butter, frowned, and tossed it into the garbage. 'That ought to do it,' she said, and put the unopened cans of soup in the cupboard. I sat at the table and watched as Helen washed the dirty dishes, tied up the garbage bag, and poured boiling water into two cups. She handed one to me without milk, and sat down at the table.

'Excuse me, Madam, but is it enough?'

Helen took a sip of her tea. Her lipstick left a smiling pink stain on the rim of the cup. 'Is what enough?'

'The soup in the pans. Is it enough food for Mrs. Croft?'

'She won't eat anything else. She stopped eating solids after she turned one hundred. That was, let's see, three years ago.'

327 vulnerable [ˈvʌlnərəbl]: *verwundbar*
332 glare (v): look angrily
337 chaperone [ˈʃæpərəʊn]: *Anstandsdame (Frau, die auf eine unverheiratete junge Frau aufpasst)*
341 station: *Stand, (gesellschaftliche) Stellung*
341 reveal sth.: *etwas verraten, etwas zeigen*
341 ankle: *Fußknöchel*
344 sniff (v): take a short breath through the nose
360 garbage [ˈgɑːbɪdʒ]: *(Küchen-)Abfälle*
369 solids [ˈsɒlɪdz] (pl): solid food

I was mortified. I had assumed Mrs. Croft was in her eighties, perhaps as old as ninety. I had never known a person who had lived for over a century. That this person was a widow who lived alone mortified me further still. Widowhood had driven my own mother insane. My father, who worked as a clerk at the General Post Office of Calcutta, died of encephalitis when I was sixteen. My mother refused to adjust to life without him; instead she sank deeper into a world of darkness from which neither I, nor my brother, nor concerned relatives, nor psychiatric clinics on Rash Behari Avenue could save her. What pained me most was to see her so unguarded, to hear her burp after meals or expel gas in front of company without the slightest embarrassment. After my father's death my brother abandoned his schooling and began to work in the jute mill he would eventually manage, in order to keep the household running. And so it was my job to sit by my mother's feet and study for my exams as she counted and recounted the bracelets on her arm as if they were the beads of an abacus. We tried to keep an eye on her. Once she had wandered half naked to the tram depot before we were able to bring her inside again.

'I am happy to warm Mrs. Croft's soup in the evenings,' I suggested. 'It is no trouble.'

Helen looked at her watch, stood up, and poured the rest of her tea into the sink. 'I wouldn't if I were you. That's the sort of thing that would kill her altogether.'

That evening, when Helen had gone and Mrs. Croft and I were alone again, I began to worry. Now that I knew how very old she was, I worried that something would happen to her in the middle of the night, or when I was out during the day. As vigorous as her voice was, and imperious as she seemed, I knew that even a scratch or a cough could kill a person that old; each day she lived, I knew, was something of a miracle. Helen didn't seem concerned. She came and went, bringing soup for Mrs. Croft, one Sunday after the next.

In this manner the six weeks of that summer passed. I came home each evening, after my hours at the library, and spent a few minutes on the piano bench with Mrs. Croft. Some evenings I sat beside her long after she had drifted off to sleep, still in awe of how many years she had spent on this earth. At times I tried to picture the world she had been born into, in 1866 – a world, I imagined, filled with women in long black skirts, and chaste conversations in the parlor. Now, when I looked at her hands with their swollen knuckles folded together in her lap, I imagined them smooth and slim, striking the piano keys. At times I came downstairs before going to sleep, to make sure she was sitting upright on the bench, or was safe in her bedroom. On Fridays I put the rent in her hands. There was nothing I could do for her beyond these simple gestures. I was not her son, and, apart from those eight dollars, I owed her nothing.

371 mortified: very embarrassed
373 widow: woman whose husband has died
374 widowhood: state of being a widow
374 drive sb. insane: *jdn. in den Wahnsinn treiben*
376 encephalitis [enˌsefəˈlaɪtɪs]: *Gehirnentzündung*
376 adjust to sth. [əˈdʒʌst]: *sich an etwas anpassen*
378 concerned: *besorgt*
380 burp: *rülpsen*
380 expel gas [ɪkˈspel]: *Darmluft abgehen lassen*
381 slight: very minor
385 bracelet [ˈbreɪslət]: *Armreif*
397 vigorous [ˈvɪɡərəs]: strong, energetic
397 imperious [ɪmˈpɪəriəs] (fml): tending to give orders to other people
398 scratch: *Kratzer*
405 be in awe of sth.: *Ehrfurcht vor etwas haben*
408 chaste (fml): *keusch*
410 slim: *schlank*

At the end of August, Mala's passport and green card were ready. I received a telegram with her flight information; my brother's house in Calcutta had no telephone. Around that time I also received a letter from her, written only a few days after we had parted. There was no salutation; addressing me by name would have assumed an intimacy we had not yet discovered. It contained only a few lines. 'I write in English in preparation for the journey. Here I am very much lonely. Is it very cold there. Is there snow. Yours, Mala.'

I was not touched by her words. We had spent only a handful of days in each other's company. And yet we were bound together; for six weeks she had worn an iron bangle on her wrist, and applied vermillion powder to the part in her hair, to signify to the world that she was a bride. In those six weeks I regarded her arrival as I would the arrival of a coming month, or season – something inevitable, but meaningless at the time. So little did I know her that, while details of her face sometimes rose to my memory, I could not conjure up the whole of it.

A few days after receiving the letter, as I was walking to work in the morning, I saw an Indian woman on Massachusetts Avenue, wearing a sari with its free end nearly dragging on the footpath, and pushing a child in a stroller. An American woman with a small black dog on a leash was walking to one side of her. Suddenly the dog began barking. I watched as the Indian woman, startled, stopped in her path, at which point the dog leaped up and seized the end of the sari between its teeth. The American woman scolded the dog, appeared to apologize, and walked quickly away, leaving the Indian woman to fix her sari, and quiet her crying child. She did not see me standing there, and eventually she continued on her way. Such a mishap, I realized that morning, would soon be my concern. It was my duty to take care of Mala, to welcome her and protect her. I would have to buy her her first pair of snow boots, her first winter coat. I would have to tell her which streets to avoid, which way the traffic came, tell her to wear her sari so that the free end did not drag on the footpath. A five-mile separation from her parents, I recalled with some irritation, had caused her to weep.

Unlike Mala, I was used to it all by then: used to cornflakes and milk, used to Helen's visits, used to sitting on the bench with Mrs. Croft. The only thing I was not used to was Mala. Nevertheless I did what I had to do. I went to the housing office at M.I.T. and found a furnished apartment a few blocks away, with a double bed and a private kitchen and bath, for forty dollars a week. One last Friday I handed Mrs. Croft eight dollar bills in an envelope, brought my suitcase downstairs, and informed her that I was moving. She put my key into her change purse. The last thing she asked me to do was hand her the cane propped against the table, so that she could walk to the door and lock it behind me. 'Goodbye, then,' she said, and retreated back into the house. I did not expect any display of emotion, but I was disappointed all the same.

420 salutation [ˌsæljuˈteɪʃn]: standard word or phrase used at the beginning of a letter
420 address sb. [əˈdres]: *jdn. ansprechen*
426 bangle: bracelet
426 wrist: *Handgelenk*
426 vermil(l)ion (adj): bright red
427 part: *Scheitel*
427 signify sth.: make sth. clear
431 conjure sth. up: [ˈkʌndʒə] imagine sth.
434 sari [ˈsɑːri]: long dress worn in India
434 drag: *schleifen*
435 stroller (AE): *Kinderwagen, Buggy*
435 leash (n): *Hundeleine*
437 startle sb.: *jdn. erschrecken*
438 leap (v): jump
438 seize sth. [siːz]: *etwas packen*
439 scold sb.: *mit jdm. schimpfen*
439 apologize [əˈpɒlədʒaɪz]: say you are sorry
442 mishap: *Missgeschick*
443 concern: task, business
451 nevertheless: *trotzdem*
452 furnished: *möbliert*
459 retreat (v): *sich zurückziehen*

I was only a boarder, a man who paid her a bit of money and passed in and out of her home for six weeks. Compared with a century, it was no time at all.

At the airport I recognized Mala immediately. The free end of her sari did not drag on the floor, but was draped in a sign of bridal modesty over her head, just as it had draped my mother until the day my father died. Her thin brown arms were stacked with gold bracelets, a small red circle was painted on her forehead, and the edges of her feet were tinted with a decorative red dye. I did not embrace her, or kiss her, or take her hand. Instead I asked her, speaking Bengali for the first time in America, if she was hungry.

She hesitated, then nodded yes.

I told her I had prepared some egg curry at home. 'What did they give you to eat on the plane?'

'I didn't eat.'

'All the way from Calcutta?'

'The menu said oxtail soup.'

'But surely there were other items.'

'The thought of eating an ox's tail made me lose my appetite.'

When we arrived home, Mala opened up one of her suitcases, and presented me with two pullover sweaters, both made with bright-blue wool, which she had knitted in the course of our separation, one with a V-neck, the other covered with cables. I tried them on; both were tight under the arms. She had also brought me two new pairs of drawstring pajamas, a letter from my brother, and a packet of loose Darjeeling tea. I had no present for her apart from the egg curry. We sat at a bare table, staring at our plates. We ate with our hands, another thing I had not yet done in America.

'The house is nice,' she said. 'Also the egg curry.' With her left hand she held the end of her sari to her chest, so it would not slip off her head.

'I don't know many recipes.'

She nodded, peeling the skin off each of her potatoes before eating them. At one point the sari slipped to her shoulders. She readjusted it at once.

'There is no need to cover your head,' I said. 'I don't mind. It doesn't matter here.'

She kept it covered anyway.

I waited to get used to her, to her presence at my side, at my table and in my bed, but a week later we were still strangers. I still was not used to coming home to an apartment that smelled of steamed rice, and finding that the basin in the bathroom was always wiped clean, our two toothbrushes lying side by side, a cake of Pears soap residing in the soap dish. I was not used to the fragrance of the coconut oil she rubbed every other night into her scalp, or the delicate sound her bracelets

465 modesty [ˈmɒdəsti]: *Sittsamkeit, Anstand*
469 dye: *Farbstoff*
469 embrace sb.: close sb. in your arms
472 hesitate [ˈhezɪteɪt]: *zögern*
483 covered with cables: *im Zopfmuster*
494 readjust sth. [ˌriːəˈdʒʌst]: *etwas ordnen oder richten*
503 Pears soap [peəz]: British brand of soap (first made in 1807)
503 reside [rɪˈzaɪd]: (here) lie
504 fragrance [ˈfreɪgrəns]: (pleasant) smell
505 every other night: *jede zweite Nacht*
505 scalp: *Kopfhaut*
505 delicate [ˈdelɪkət]: soft

made as she moved about the apartment. In the mornings she was always awake before I was. The first morning when I came into the kitchen she had heated up the leftovers and set a plate with a spoonful of salt on its edge, assuming I would eat rice for breakfast, as most Bengali husbands did. I told her cereal would do, and the next morning when I came into the kitchen she had already poured the cornflakes into my bowl. One morning she walked with me to M.I.T., where I gave her a short tour of the campus. The next morning before I left for work she asked me for a few dollars. I parted with them reluctantly, but I knew that this, too, was now normal. When I came home from work there was a potato peeler in the kitchen drawer, and a tablecloth on the table, and chicken curry made with fresh garlic and ginger on the stove. After dinner I read the newspaper, while Mala sat at the kitchen table, working on a cardigan for herself with more of the blue wool, or writing letters home.

On Friday, I suggested going out. Mala set down her knitting and disappeared into the bathroom. When she emerged I regretted the suggestion; she had put on a silk sari and extra bracelets, and coiled her hair with a flattering side part on top of her head. She was prepared as if for a party, or at the very least for the cinema, but I had no such destination in mind. The evening was balmy. We walked several blocks down Massachusetts Avenue, looking into the windows of restaurants and shops. Then, without thinking, I led her down the quiet street where for so many nights I had walked alone.

'This is where I lived before you came,' I said, stopping at Mrs. Croft's chain-link fence.

'In such a big house?'

'I had a small room upstairs. At the back.'

'Who else lives there?'

'A very old woman.'

'With her family?'

'Alone.'

'But who takes care of her?'

I opened the gate. 'For the most part she takes care of herself.'

I wondered if Mrs. Croft would remember me; I wondered if she had a new boarder to sit with her each evening. When I pressed the bell I expected the same long wait as that day of our first meeting, when I did not have a key. But this time the door was opened almost immediately, by Helen. Mrs. Croft was not sitting on the bench. The bench was gone.

'Hello there,' Helen said, smiling with her bright pink lips at Mala. 'Mother's in the parlor. Will you be visiting awhile?'

'As you wish, Madam.'

'Then I think I'll run to the store, if you don't mind. She had a little accident. We can't leave her alone these days, not even for a minute.'

508 leftovers (pl): food left over from an earlier meal
514 reluctantly [rɪˈlʌktəntli]: *ungern, widerwillig*
516 potato peeler: *Kartoffelschäler*
517 garlic: *Knoblauch*
517 ginger [ˈdʒɪndʒə]: *Ingwer*
519 cardigan [ˈkɑːdɪgən]: *Strickjacke*
522 emerge [ɪˈmɜːdʒ]: reappear
526 destination: *Ziel(ort)*
526 balmy [ˈbɑːmi]: *mild*

I locked the door after Helen and walked into the parlor. Mrs. Croft was lying flat on her back, her head on a peach-colored cushion, a thin white quilt spread over her body. Her hands were folded together on her chest. When she saw me she pointed at the sofa, and told me to sit down. I took my place as directed, but Mala wandered over to the piano and sat on the bench, which was now positioned where it belonged.

'I broke my hip!' Mrs. Croft announced, as if no time had passed.

'Oh dear, Madam.'

'I fell off the bench!'

'I am so sorry, Madam.'

'It was the middle of the night! Do you know what I did, boy?'

I shook my head.

'I called the police!'

She stared up at the ceiling and grinned sedately, exposing a crowded row of long gray teeth. 'What do you say to that, boy?'

As stunned as I was, I knew what I had to say. With no hesitation at all, I cried out, 'Splendid!'

Mala laughed then. Her voice was full of kindness, her eyes bright with amusement. I had never heard her laugh before, and it was loud enough so that Mrs. Croft heard, too. She turned to Mala and glared.

'Who is she, boy?'

'She is my wife, Madam.'

Mrs. Croft pressed her head at an angle against the cushion to get a better look. 'Can you play the piano?'

'No, Madam,' Mala replied.

'Then stand up!'

Mala rose to her feet, adjusting the end of her sari over her head and holding it to her chest, and, for the first time since her arrival, I felt sympathy. I remembered my first days in London, learning how to take the Tube to Russell Square, riding an escalator for the first time, unable to understand that when the man cried 'piper' it meant 'paper', unable to decipher, for a whole year, that the conductor said 'Mind the gap' as the train pulled away from each station. Like me, Mala had travelled far from home, not knowing where she was going, or what she would find, for no reason other than to be my wife. As strange as it seemed, I knew in my heart that one day her death would affect me, and stranger still, that mine would affect her. I wanted somehow to explain this to Mrs. Croft, who was still scrutinizing Mala from top to toe with what seemed to be placid disdain. I wondered if Mrs. Croft had ever seen a woman in a sari, with a dot painted on her forehead and bracelets stacked on her wrists. I wondered what she would object to. I wondered if she could see the red dye still vivid on Mala's feet, all but obscured by the bottom edge of her sari. At last Mrs. Croft declared, with the equal measures of disbelief and delight I knew well:

'She is a perfect lady!'

551 peach: *Pfirsich*
551 cushion [ˈkʊʃn]: *Kissen*
552 quilt: *Steppdecke*
563 sedate [sɪˈdeɪt]: calm
563 expose sth. [ɪkˈspəʊz]: make sth. visible
565 stun sb.: shock sb.
572 at an angle [ˈæŋgl]: *angewinkelt*
579 escalator [ˈeskəleɪtə]: moving staircase
581 decipher sth. [dɪˈsaɪfə]: discover the meaning of sth.
581 conductor [kənˈdʌktə]: station attendant
585 affect sb. [əˈfekt]: *jdm. nahegehen*
587 scrutinize sb.: examine sb. closely
588 placid [ˈplæsɪd]: calm
588 disdain (n): *Verachtung*
590 object to sth. [əbˈdʒekt]: be against sth.
591 vivid [ˈvɪvɪd]: bright
591 obscure sth.: hide sth. from view

Now it was I who laughed. I did so quietly, and Mrs. Croft did not hear me. But Mala had heard, and, for the first time, we looked at each other and smiled.

I like to think of that moment in Mrs. Croft's parlor as the moment when the distance between Mala and me began to lessen. Although we were not yet fully in love, I like to think of the months that followed as a honeymoon of sorts. Together we explored the city and met other Bengalis, some of whom are still friends today. We discovered that a man named Bill sold fresh fish on Prospect Street, and that a shop in Harvard Square called Cardullo's sold bay leaves and cloves. In the evenings we walked to the Charles River to watch sailboats drift across the water, or had ice-cream cones in Harvard Yard. We bought a camera with which to document our life together, and I took pictures of her posing in front of the Prudential Building, so that she could send them to her parents. At night we kissed, shy at first but quickly bold, and discovered pleasure and solace in each other's arms. I told her about my voyage on the S. S. Roma, and about Finsbury Park and the Y. M. C. A., and my evenings on the bench with Mrs. Croft. When I told her stories about my mother, she wept. It was Mala who consoled me when, reading the Globe one evening, I came across Mrs. Croft's obituary. I had not thought of her in several months – by then those six weeks of the summer were already a remote interlude in my past – but when I learned of her death I was stricken, so much so that when Mala looked up from her knitting she found me staring at the wall, unable to speak. Mrs. Croft's was the first death I mourned in America, for hers was the first life I had admired; she had left this world at last, ancient and alone, never to return.

As for me, I have not strayed much farther. Mala and I live in a town about twenty miles from Boston, on a tree-lined street much like Mrs. Croft's, in a house we own, with room for guests, and a garden that saves us from buying tomatoes in summer. We are American citizens now, so that we can collect Social Security when it is time. Though we visit Calcutta every few years, we have decided to grow old here. I work in a small college library. We have a son who attends Harvard University. Mala no longer drapes the end of her sari over her head, or weeps at night for her parents, but occasionally she weeps for our son. So we drive to Cambridge to visit him, or bring him home for a weekend, so that he can eat rice with us with his hands, and speak in Bengali, things we sometimes worry he will no longer do after we die.

Whenever we make that drive, I always take Massachusetts Avenue, in spite of the traffic. I barely recognize the buildings now, but each time I am there I return instantly to those six weeks as if they were only the other day, and I slow down and point to Mrs. Croft's street, saying to my son, Here was my first home in America, where I lived with a woman who was a hundred and three. 'Remember?' Mala says, and

599 lessen: become less
604 bay leaves (pl): *Lorbeerbätter*
604 clove [kləʊv]: *Gewürznelke*
606 cone: *(Eis-)Waffel*
609 bold: unafraid
610 solace ['sɒləs] (n, fml): *Trost*
614 obituary [əˈbɪtʃuəri]: *Todesanzeige*
616 interlude ['ɪntəluːd]: *Zwischenspiel*
617 stricken (fml): *betroffen*
619 mourn sb.'s death [mɔːn] (fml): feel sorrow because sb. has died
620 admire sth. [ədˈmaɪə]: *etwas bewundern*
622 stray (v): wander
626 Social Security: state pension for retired people in the USA
636 instantly ['ɪnstəntli]: at once
637 the other day: a few days ago

smiles, amazed, as I am, that there was ever a time that we were strangers. My son always expresses his astonishment, not at Mrs. Croft's age but at how little I paid in rent, a fact nearly as inconceivable to him as a flag on the moon was to a woman born in 1866. In my son's eyes I see the ambition that had first hurled me across the world. In a few years he will graduate and pave his own way, alone and unprotected. But I remind myself that he has a father who is still living, a mother who is happy and strong. Whenever he is discouraged, I tell him that if I can survive on three continents, then there is no obstacle he cannot conquer. While the astronauts, heroes forever, spent mere hours on the moon, I have remained in this new world for nearly thirty years. I know that my achievement is quite ordinary. I am not the only man to seek his fortune far from home, and certainly I am not the first. Still, there are times I am bewildered by each mile I have travelled, each meal I have eaten, each person I have known, each room in which I have slept. As ordinary as it all appears, there are times when it is beyond my imagination.

From: Interpreter of Maladies (Stories), *1999, Houghton Mifflin Harcourt, pp. 173ff.*

642 inconceivable [ˌɪnkənˈsiːvəbl]: unimaginable
644 hurl sth.: throw sth.
645 graduate [ˈɡrædʒueɪt] (v): complete your high school or university education
645 pave your own way: find your own way in life
647 discouraged: *entmutigt*
648 obstacle [ˈɒbstəkl]: sth. that is in your way
648 conquer sth. [ˈkɒŋkə]: *etwas überwinden*
649 mere (adj): (here) only
653 bewildered [bɪˈwɪldəd]: confused

Info Jhumpa Lahiri

Nilanjana Sudeshna Lahiri was born in London (UK) in 1967. Her parents were both from the Bengali region in India. When she was three years old, her family moved to the US, where her father got a job as a librarian at the University of Rhode Island in Kingston. His biography mirrors that of the narrator in 'The Third and Final Continent'. Lahiri's nickname *Jhumpa* became her usual name when she entered kindergarten due to teachers having trouble remembering her proper name. Lahiri graduated with a B.A. in literature from Columbia University in 1989. She also has an M.A. and a Ph.D. from Boston College. Her first successful publication was the anthology of short stories *Interpreter of Maladies* (1999), which brought her national attention. She has since written a second collection of short stories and three novels. Most of her work focuses on the lives of Indian Americans.

Comprehension

1 Outline the events of the narrator's life in chronological order.

Analysis

2 Examine the relationship between the narrator and his wife Mala. Analyse how it changes in the course of the story.

3 **a** Compare the way the narrator presents Mrs. Croft and his own mother.

b Analyse the role Mrs. Croft plays in the narrator's life.

4 Examine how the narrator and Mala adapt to life in the USA.

5 Explain the meaning of the title with regard to the narrator's biography.

Beyond the text

6 **Writing** Describe the final visit to Mrs. Croft's house (ll. 550–597) from Mala's point of view.

7 Take a look at the graph and complete the eight sentences below.

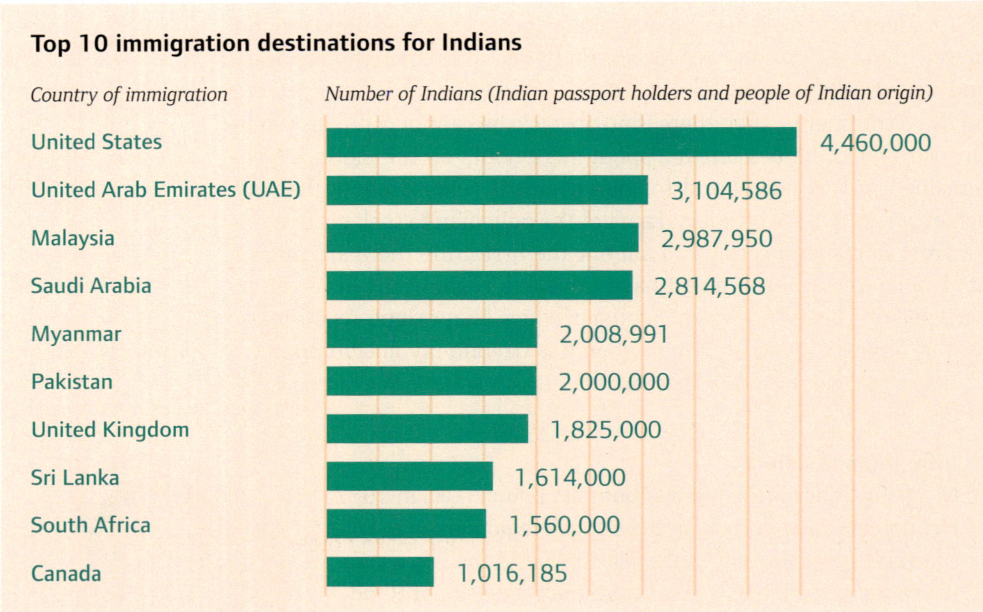

Data from Ministry of External Affairs India and Pew Research Center (Pakistan Data)

A ________________ Indians live in the UK ________________ in Sri Lanka.

B Nearly twice ________________ Indians live in Myanmar ________________ in Canada.

C The Indian population of South Africa is roughly ________________ that of the UAE.

D The USA is the country with ________________ Indians outside of India.

E Saudi Arabia is the ____________ popular country of immigration for Indians living abroad.

F The Indian populations of Myanmar and Pakistan are almost ________________.

G ________________ Indians live in South Africa ________________ in Saudi Arabia.

H The ________________ popular country of immigration on the list is Canada.

8 Comparing the countries in the graph, speculate on the pull factors that make these destinations attractive for Indians going abroad. Refer also to the narrator's choices in Lahiri's story.

9 Comment on the following statement. Refer to Lahiri's story as an example.

Successful integration means adapting to your new surroundings as much as necessary while retaining your identity as much as possible.

Info The Indian diaspora
Ever since the UN started following international migration trends in 1990, India has ranked as one of the world's leading sources of migrant labour. In 2019, the Indian diaspora (i. e. the group of Indians living abroad) was estimated at 17.5 million. At present, the most popular destinations for Indian emigrants are the United Arab Emirates, the USA and Pakistan. In the USA, India is the third-largest country of origin of new immigrants (after Mexico and China). In Canada, India is the second-biggest source of newcomers. Indians living in North America tend to be well-educated and economically successful. The UK also has a sizeable Indian-born population, due in part to the close connection between Britain and its former colony.

B4 'The Escape' *Qaisra Shahraz*

1 a Think: How would you define the term 'home'? Make notes.
b Speaking **Pair:** Get together with a partner and discuss your answers to the question in **a**.
c Speaking **Share:** Discuss the points you agreed and disagreed on with the class.

Read the short story and complete the tasks on pp. 62–66.

In the packed prayer hall of Darul Uloom mosque in Longsight, the Imam concluded the Eid prayers with a passionate plea for world peace and terrorist activities in Pakistan to stop. Seventy-three-year-old Samir, perched on a plastic chair because of his bad leg, kept his hands raised, quietly mouthing his own personal prayer.

'Please, Allah Pak, bless her soul! And let me escape!'

Rows of seated men had arisen from their prayer mats and reached out to energetically hug others and offer the festive greeting, 'Eid Mubarak!' Samir took his time. There was no one in particular he was seeking to greet or hug at this mosque. Most of the men around him were strangers and of the younger generation, several sporting beards – a marked shift between the two generations. His face remained clean-shaven. Nowadays he prayed at the Cheadle mosque, joining the congregation of Arabs and other nationalities for the Taraveeh prayers during Ramadhan. Nostalgia tugging at him, on a whim, Samir had asked his son to drop him off in Longsight to offer his Eid prayers at his old community mosque.

2 Eid [iːd]: Muslim holiday (festival of breaking the fast)
6 Allah Pak: religious address
14 congregation: religious community
15 on a whim: spontaneously

Chana chaat

Painfully rising to his feet Samir began the hugging ritual, smiling cordially. Unlike the others leaving the hall, he loitered; in no hurry to get out. At the door he dutifully dropped a five-pound note in the collection fund box.

Whilst looking for his shoes, he bumped into his old friend, Manzoor – they greeted, smiled broadly and warmly hugged. Outside, in the chilly autumn day, his friend, who lived a street away from the mosque, invited him to his house for the Eid hospitality of *Vermicelles*, *Seviyan* and *chana chaat*.

The smile slid off Samir's face; he was reluctant to visit his friend's house – afraid of the old memories, shying away from the normality, the marital bliss of his friend's home. In particular he was loath to witness the little intimacies between husband and wife. The look. The laugh. The teasing banter.

Instead he waved goodbye to his friend and stood waiting for his son. 'I'm being picked up,' he informed a young man kindly offering him a lift home, before sauntering on his bad leg down the street.

'I have all the time in the world!' he wryly muttered to himself, savouring the walk down streets he had cycled and scooted along for over three decades. A lot had changed, the area now thriving with different migrant communities; the Pakistanis and the Bengalis living side by side with the Irish and the Somalis. Many Asian stores and shops had sprung up. The Bengali Sari and travel-agent shops jostled happily alongside the Pakistani ones and the Chinese takeaway. Mosques catering to the needs of Muslim community had sprung up, from the small Duncan Road mosque in a semi-detached corner house to the purpose-built Darul Uloom centre on Stamford Road. The Bengali mosque for the Bengali community on one corner of Buller Road was only a few feet away from the Pakistani and Arab Makki Masjid on the other corner. Not surprisingly on Fridays, for the *Juma* prayers, the street was gridlocked, with an occasional police car monitoring the situation.

He noted that the Roman Catholic church and its primary school on Montgomery Road had disappeared, joining the quaint little National Westminister Bank branch that had been in the middle of Beresford Road with a communal vegetable plot at the back. That had been pulled down twenty-odd years ago. St Agnes Church was still there, however, at the junction of West Point and Hamilton Road and it still enjoyed healthy Sunday morning gatherings.

Samir stopped outside a shop on Beresford Road that had been called Joy Town twenty-one years earlier. It had been his children's favourite toyshop, especially on Eid day, when they ran to it with their *Eidhi* money, eager to buy cars, skipping ropes and doll's china crockery sets. In its place there now stood a grocery superstore with stalls of vegetables and fruits hogging the pavement area. On Fridays and Saturdays

19 loiter: hang around, wait aimlessly
25 hospitality [ˌhɒspɪˈtæləti]: *Gastfreundschaft*
25–26 *Vermicelles* [ˌvɜːmɪˈtʃeliz], *sewayian*, *chana chaat*: Pakistani specialities
34 saunter [ˈsɔːntə] (v): walk in a relaxed way
36 savour sth. [ˈseɪvə]: enjoy sth., taste sth.
48 gridlocked (adj): blocked
51 quaint: *altmodisch anmutend*
62 hog sth. (infml): fill sth. up

families, like Samir's, who had moved out of the area still returned to do their shopping, visiting their favourite halal meat and grocery stores; carting boxes of fresh mangoes, bags of basmati rice and chappati flour back to their cars. The hustle and bustle of these shops always bought out a smile in him.

His son, Maqbool, a well-to-do sportswear manager, dutifully returned to pick him up half an hour later. By that time Samir was shivering with the autumn chill in his *shalwar kameze* and *sherwani* and gladly got into the warm car. He had wanted to go to Sanam Sweet Centre to buy a few boxes of Asian sweets to distribute to friends but he hesitated, suddenly overcome by trepidation.

'Do you want to go somewhere else, Father?' his son asked, as if reading his mind.

Samir shook his head; loath to inconvenience his son further, feeling guilty for already taking up enough of his time.

'No. Let's go home,' he murmured, eyes closed.

He had a large five-bedroom detached house but, with his wife and family gone, all the joy of living had fled. He kept himself in the master bedroom, hating to enter the other rooms in the house, especially the one with his wife's clothes. Only when the grandchildren visited did he unlock some of the doors. He spent his time in his new favourite spot, the chair at the dining table next to the window and radiator. He sat there leafing through *The Times*, the *Daily Jang* and *The Nation*, watching the traffic go past on the busy road.

His son dropped him off at the door with the words, 'Will collect you in an hour's time.' Samir nodded and watched him drive away before letting himself into the house. Another hour to kill. He shrugged. It was better here on his own, with the TV and the newspaper keeping him company, than politely waiting around at someone else's house for dinner.

He felt hungry; but the dining table in front of him lay dismally bare. On Eid days it was normally stacked with bowls of delicious food: boiled eggs, *Seviyan*, *chana chaat* and a hot tray of Shami kebabs. And these were just the breakfast starters, heralding a busy festive day of eating.

Last year his entire family had been there. If he closed his eyes he could see his children helping themselves to the food, with him happily beginning the Eidhi money-giving ritual. Five-pound notes for the little ones, ten for the older teenagers, and crispy twenty-pound notes for his daughters and daughters-in-law.

In the steamy warm kitchen with the noisy fan purring away at the window, the smell from a pot of pilau rice and trays of roast chicken and kebabs in the oven would set everyone's mouth watering. Dinner was a prompt affair; always at one o'clock, served by the women of his household, moving elegantly around the room; their rustling *ghararas* and *lenghas* sweeping the floor and the long *dupattas* hanging at their

64 halal [hə'læl, hə'lɑːl] (adj): (of food) religiously correct
66 hustle and bustle: *Gedränge*
70 *shalwar kameze* [ʃʌl'wɑː kə'miːz], *sherwani* [ʃɜː'wɑːni]: traditional Pakistani clothing
73 trepidation [ˌtrepɪ'deɪʃn]: worry about sth. unpleasant that might happen
76 inconvenience sb. [ˌɪnkən'viːniəns] (fml): be a burden to sb.
79 detached house: *frei stehendes Haus, Einzelhaus*
84 radiator ['reɪdieɪtə]: *Heizung*
93 dismal ['dɪzməl]: miserable, gloomy
96 herald sth. ['herəld] (fml): announce sth.
106–107 *gharara* [gə'rɑːrə], *lengha*: traditional Pakistani women's clothing
107 *dupatta* [dʊ'pʌtə]: shawl, traditional Pakistani clothing

Shami kebabs

A dupatta (left) and lengha

sides. The boys would be in their *shalwar kameze* and *sherwanis*. By two, the whole family would be sitting around the table chatting, relaxed and happy, some still spooning away trifle and *gajar halwa*.

The thought of all that food set Samir's stomach groaning. He could not wait that long. In the kitchen he tipped some cornflakes into a bowl; it was not *chana chaat* or *Seviyan* but would keep him going.

He twice checked his pocket for the money, mentally counting the number of notes he should have. This was the bit of Eid day that he particularly enjoyed, glimpsing the excited faces of his grandchildren taking the Eidhi from his hand. In the old days a one-pound coin delighted his children. After dinner they excitedly ran off to Joy Town to buy gifts of their choice.

When Maqbool arrived, Samir was well into his second hard-boiled egg, smiling sheepishly at his son, who mentally chided himself for leaving his father to eat alone at home.

Samir's whole family was gathered in his eldest daughter's house and he was the last to arrive. In the living room his second daughter-in-law, Mehnaz, stood up out of respect to vacate her seat for him.

'Stay seated, my dear,' he offered, perching himself instead on a chair near the door. The women were busy in the kitchen, sorting out the crockery and the sauces. All had happily adopted the British custom of bringing a dish since their mother had died. His eldest daughter was carrying a tray of roast meat through the hallway to the dining room. Catching her eye, Samir smiled politely.

His youngest grandson Rahel jumped into his lap, startling him and bringing a smile to his face. Samir lifted him up to offer a tight hug. Then holding out a five-pound note he beckoned to his older grandson, a six-year-old, who was stood scowling a few feet away. The child shyly sidled to his grandfather's side, plucked the note from his hand and ran off.

'Would you like something to eat before dinner?' His daughter came to enquire, the blender with the mint sauce in her hand.

Samir shook his head.

Nodding, she disappeared into the kitchen, leaving Samir to smile, watch, listen and respond where appropriate. That is until the seat became too uncomfortable for his bad leg, forcing him to take the one vacated by his eldest grandson near the window. He bleakly stared out through the net curtains, watching passers-by, who probably had no idea that in this Muslim home they were celebrating Eid ul-Fitr.

Eyes filling up, Samir kept his face averted towards the window; there was nothing to celebrate on his first Eid without his beloved wife. Sorrow suffocated; desperation tearing at him. If he could only turn the clock back. How he longed to have this Eid dinner at his own home and with her hosting it; instead of sitting awkwardly here as an interloper.

An hour later he dutifully spooned food into his mouth; making no comments apart from the polite 'everything is very nice' to the women

Man wearing a sherwani and dupatta

110 trifle: cold dessert made from cake covered with fruit
110 *gajar halwa*: sweet dessert pudding with carrots
121 chide yourself (fml): criticize yourself, blame yourself
132 startle sb.: surprise sb.
134 beckon to sb.: make an inviting gesture to sb.
135 scowl [skaʊl] (v): look at sb. in an angry or annoyed way
146 avert your face [əˈvɜːt]: turn your face away from sth.
148 sorrow: great sadness, grief
150 interloper [ˈɪntələʊpə]: intruder

of his family. He did not pick on the chillis or criticise the curry sauces as he had always done with his wife's cooking. His sons, of a different generation and attitude, were happily munching away at their roast meats, whilst he stealthily hid a raw bit of chicken leg under a napkin on his plate.

By the time the *gajar halwa* and tea were served, Samir's mind was made up. He waited; heartbeat accelerating. When there was a lull in the lively conversation, he ventured to inform his family, licking his dry lips carefully.

'I want to tell you something ...'

They turned to stare. His daughter Roxanna hushed her little girl sitting on her lap with the words, 'Abu ji is speaking, shush!'

'I want to go back home – to Pakistan,' Samir announced, 'To visit my family ... stay there for a few months. It'll be good for me ... it's the right time ... with your mother gone ... I need a change of scene and I have plenty of time now!' he explained, smiling. 'It would be lovely to visit some places of my old life. Also good to spend some time with my sister and brother and their families.' Complete silence greeted his words.

'A few months! Are you sure about this, father? We'll miss you!' His eldest daughter had found her tongue.

'You'll all be fine without me. Anyway you can phone me every day ... you've all got busy lives and families, so it won't be that bad to have me disappear for a few months. I'll hardly be missed ... This trip will be good for me ... I need to go ...' He stopped himself from saying, 'I need to escape,' voice petering away, giving them a glimpse of the abyss inside him.

Discomforted and not knowing what was the right thing to say, they prudently ended the discussion. Their father had always made his own decisions – very rarely paying any attention to other people's opinions. Their mother had battled for years to influence him, and died having never quite succeeded.

'Where will you stay? Lahore?' his youngest daughter Rosie boldly asked.

'Yes! In our family home of course, with my brother – where else?' he replied sharply, annoyed at his daughter's question and semi-hostile tone.

Rosie did not bother answering. Instead she covertly exchanged a pointed look with her sister, which their father neatly intercepted. Samir's face tightened. 'You need to understand, Rosie, that just as this is your family – I have the same back home ... They care about me and want me to spend time with them.' His tone harsher than he intended.

The word 'back home' had just slipped out of him again. It was a curious use. For a few seconds he was lost in thought. Why did he say that? Was Manchester not his 'home'? After all he had spent over forty

159 lull (n): pause
164 Abu ji: familiar address, grandfather
178 peter away = peter out: *sich verlieren, abklingen*
179 abyss [əˈbɪs]: *Abgrund*
180 discomforted [dɪsˈkʌmfətɪd] (fml): *in Verlegenheit gebracht*
181 prudent [ˈpruːdnt] (fml): wise
188–189 semi-hostile [ˌsemiˈhɒstaɪl]: *halb feindlich*
191 intercept sth.: *etwas abfangen*

years of his life in this city. The other place was just his birthplace, his country of origin and reminder of his youth. Surely these facts should make Manchester his home.

He shrugged these thoughts aside, willing his mood to lighten; he had a goal: to preoccupy his mind with tasks, and he loved tasks above all. The big task facing him now was what presents to take for his family and his two college friends in Lahore. He promised himself that this time the three friends would treat themselves to a walk through the tall elegant Victorian corridors of the Government College of Lahore where he had studied.

Three days later, Samir had flown out from Manchester airport, taking his 'other family' in Lahore by surprise. They gushed with greetings, hurriedly assembling their shocked faces even though inside they were all amok. 'What was he doing here, all of sudden? How long was he going to stay? Which other relatives was he visiting and for how long?' These questions battered simultaneously in all their heads.

Samir's face fell, quickly averting his eyes, astutely picking up the telltale signs from their faces and body language. Two days later, after visiting the local Anarkali Bazaar, taking a leisurely walk down the famous Mall Road, and spending time with his sister's family in her villa in the Defence area, he headed for the village where his parents were buried. There he was amicably greeted by his host, a second cousin, who hosted all relatives visiting his parents' graves.

After some refreshments Samir headed for the cemetery on the outskirts of the village. Well maintained, tall tangle wood bushes grew around it keeping the wolves out. Eyes blurred, Samir gazed down at his parents' graves. His father had adamantly made it clear that he did not want to be buried in the overcrowded city cemeteries. 'I want fresh air, shade of a tree and plenty of space around – and make sure you leave space for your mother. Don't just throw us in any hole!'

As obedient sons they honoured their father's wish and duly visited the village of their father's ancestral home and bought a plot of land. Thereafter his sister and brother made annual journeys to the village, to offer a feast and hatham prayers for their parents' souls.

Samir perched himself on the low wall circling the plot with his parents' graves. The tranquillity around him had him thinking about his own burial place. Of course it would be Manchester's Southern Cemetery. He could not imagine his children traipsing back to Pakistan to visit his grave in a land that was foreign to them. He now understood why his father was insistent on keeping a place for his wife. Remembering his Sabiya, he bowed his head. The loneliness crushed. He ached to have her back. Two years ago they were both here, sitting at the same spot.

He watched a herd of milk buffaloes being shepherded back to the village. Feeling a tiny bite, he looked down at a line of ants running down the brickwork. Laden with small scraps of leaves, the ants were

206 Government College of Lahore: university founded by the British in the mid-19th century
209–210 gush with greetings: (here) express greetings with enthusiasm that does not seem sincere
213 batter (v): hit around
214 astute [əˈstjuːt]: very clever, shrewd
215 telltale (adj): *verräterisch*
223 blurred (adj): *verschwommen, eingetrübt*
224 adamant [ˈædəmənt]: determined not to change your mind
228 obedient [əˈbiːdiənt]: doing what you are told to do
229 ancestral home [ænˈsestrəl]: *Stammsitz der Familie*
231 hatham prayer: Urdu/Pakistani Muslim prayer *(Gebet)* for a person who has died
233 tranquility [træŋˈkwɪləti]: peacefulness
235 traipse [treɪps]: walk slowly and unwillingly
242 ant: *Ameise*

zigzagging around his feet. He moved his foot away and glanced over his shoulders at the brick-making quarry and kiln, spotting a group of peasant men pushing trolleys stacked with bricks. Two women were carrying small baskets loaded with baked bricks on their heads. Feeling sorry for them and the hard work that the women had to do in order to feed their families, Samir was reminded of the second mission that had brought him to this village – his wife's charitable work. He had to visit the widow.

He turned to look back at the graves, taking his fill, etching the picture in his head. Was this going to be his final farewell? Standing over his mother's grave, soft sobs shook his large body. It was a strange world. To be buried continents away from one's own parents. Why was he crying? For his parents who had died decades ago or for his beloved Sabiya?

'Life is a cycle!' he mused. He was in his seventies but still demurred from being called 'old.' God only knew where the rest of his ancestors were buried – most probably in India, before the partition. People were born and slid through the cycle of life and then disappeared, with some leaving no trace.

'Samir, stop thinking like this – it's morbid!'

He raised his hands to say a final fervent prayer over his parents' mounds.

His host family had gone to a lot of trouble in their offer of hospitality. The women had begun scurrying around the courtyard the moment he arrived. A hen had been snatched from the chicken coop in the far end of the courtyard and quickly dispatched to the cooking pot. The rice for the lamb biryani had been soaked. The pink custard powder was energetically whisked in a bowl. Not content with the home cooking for their special 'velati' guest from 'London,' the host had enlisted the help of the village cook. A fabulous chef, it was widely said that people always licked their fingers after eating his tasty chicken shorba.

The women had happily obliged. Mina, the daughter-in-law, was seven months pregnant, expecting her first child, and hated squatting on the floor whilst cooking on a pedestal stove. As well as that, she had to maintain her modesty; it was quite challenging, keeping herself well draped in front of the male guest. Her pregnancy was causing her a lot of embarrassment. She was 'huge,' everyone kept telling her.

With a last lingering glance at his parents' graves, Samir followed the path to the village central square with its old majestic-looking Minar tree where his driver was waiting. His brother had kindly loaned both their driver and the car for his use whilst he used his motorcycle. Ahead of him he saw a young man pulling a suitcase and dragging something else.

Bemused Samir stared wide-eyed, temporarily transported to another time and place. He still kept his bedroll canvas bag in his garage in

244 brick: block of clay used for building
244 quarry [ˈkwɒri]: *Steinbruch*
244 kiln: *Brennofen*
249 charitable [ˈtʃærətəbl]: helping people who are poor or in need
251 etch sth.: draw sth.
262 morbid [ˈmɔːbɪd]: expressing a strong interest in sad or unpleasant things, especially death
263 fervent [ˈfɜːvənt]: *inbrünstig, glühend*
264 mounds (pl): (here) graves
266 scurry (v): run with quick short steps
270 whisk sth.: mix sth.
275 squat [skwɒt] (v): sit on your heels
276 pedestal stove [ˈpedɪstl]: *auf einem Sockel stehender Herd*
277 modesty [ˈmɒdəsti]: *Sittsamkeit-, Anstand*
278 drape sth. (v): hang clothes loosely
280 lingering [ˈlɪŋɡərɪŋ] (adj): not willing to leave

England, never having had the heart to throw it away. It was a memento, a part of his life. Too many memories were caught up with it. The frayed brown leather suitcase, stuffed with all his important documents, including his British nationality, was still kept under his bed.

There are special moments etched on people's minds; for Samir it was the one of him dragging a big bedroll and a large suitcase from Victoria coach station through the streets of London, deeply mortifying to this day. Why his arm and fingers did not fall off still amazed him. Tired, hungry and harassed, he and his friend stumbled thankfully into a Victorian house with a Bed and Breakfast sign; two Pakistani migrants from up north wanting to try their fortunes down south in London.

It was actually his friend's breezy confidence, smart use of English, cocky winsome smile and flirtatious winks that had successfully got them a room late at night, winning over the elegant old lady with her purple rinse. The purple hair colour of many older women in those early days fascinated him. Why did they like such a strange colour?

Samir shuddered, tasting the raw fear he had felt then as they desperately sought a place for the night. 'What if we don't find a room, where will we go and what will we do?' He had silently agonised, panicking at the darkness falling around them. It was his friend's optimism and high spirits that had saved him from making a fool of himself. There was a moment he was ready to squat on the pavement and shed bitter tears, bewailing his stupidity in leaving a warm room and a cosy bed in Blackburn.

Sharing a double bed with his friend capped the humiliation of that day further. His friend had joked at their sleeping quarters and went to sleep soundly. Samir had sidled to the edge of the bed, shivering in the thin, coarse blanket making his face itch, afraid to pull it over himself and of waking his friend. In the end he had got up and pulled out his own five-inch thick Pakistani quilt from the bedroll.

His love affair with the English capital was both doomed and short-lived – it was not for him – too anonymous. He knew no one and felt shy and uncomfortable wherever he went – stumbling and stammering over the carefully chosen English words and phrases he had mastered to buy bus tickets, packets of Benson & Hedges or order something to eat. Intimidated by the huge buildings and mad evening traffic, he smiled when he saw brown faces, mainly of Sikhs and Indians. He did not come across many Pakistanis.

After taking some souvenir photographs with an expensive camera he had brought from Pakistan, posing in his smart suit in front of one of the Trafalgar Square lions and outside the queen's Buckingham Palace gates with the guards, Samir had happily fled. He wished his friend well with his love of London. Years later when he came across him he laughed aloud. His friend had become a true Londoner, down to the cockney accent.

289 frayed (adj): *ausgefranst, abgenutzt*
300 cocky (infml): very confident
300 winsome: pleasant, attractive
300 wink (n): action of closing and opening one eye quickly, usually as a signal to sb.
302 rinse [rɪns] (n): *Haartönung, Haarspülung*
306 agonise ['ægənaɪz]: worry
310 bewail sth. (fml): express great sadness about sth.
315 itch: *jucken*
317 quilt: cover for a bed
318 doomed: *zum Scheitern verurteilt*
323 intimidated [ɪn'tɪmɪdeɪtɪd]: frightened
332 cockney: speaking like a person from the East End of London

For Samir, London was simply too much, making his life a misery and stripping away his self-esteem. Lacking his friend's confidence, easy-going manner and ability to make new friends, Samir missed the cosy comfort of a small town like Blackburn. After two weeks he had escaped, happily dragging his bedroll and his brown leather suitcase with him.

He went to another friend, who welcomed him with open arms, letting him join two other tenants in his two-bedroom terraced house. Apart from the kitchen all three rooms were used. Even the front room had a single bed hogging the area near the window and the open coal fire. That was the owner's room. The kitchen, with its big coal fire warming the room, was the hub of their communal life, where they took turns cooking meals, smoking and chatting, lounging on hard wooden chairs around a small kitchen wooden table. Three of them had young families in Pakistan.

Samir stayed put, intent on earning money to support his family back home by doing overtime and long shifts. Cooking *keema lobia* became his favourite dish. He became a good cook, very proud of his culinary skills. His first chappati painstakingly rolled with a long empty sterilised milk bottle was a good try. His three fellow home mates praised him heartily, rewarding him with the teasing words, 'Your cooking is better than our wives' back home!'

His landlord found him a job in the cotton textile mill, after he was pressured to turn down a job in a special nursing home in Darwen.

'You will be working with mentally ill people, are you mad? You'll become mad yourself!' his fellow tenants had cruelly scoffed, frightening him into scurrying into the reception room and leaving a hurried note to say no to the job before he had even started.

In the Darwen textile mill the huge dark machines intimidated him, but he quickly mastered the skill of working with and around them. It was dull and demeaning work. With his good education behind him, he often heard himself dryly echoing 'If Abba sees me doing this, he'll have a fit!' His father had forked out a lot of money for the fees for a top college and expected him to do a 'clean' respectable office job, not working in some 'grotty' mill as his youngest son once termed it years later.

The pay packet, however, had kept him smiling. The thrill of counting the banknotes through the little top corner, and feeling the angles of the six- and threepenny bits through the brown paper, and the occasional half-crowns – small sums but mighty big pleasures they provided then.

In those frugal days they felt duty-bound to keep each other in check; the talk then was always about 'going back home'. They were not here to waste money on luxuries or on themselves. Exceptions were only made for gifts for their children. Samir had not only his wife and one

334 lack sth.: not have sth.
339 tenant ['tenənt]: person who pays rent
339 terraced house [ˌterəst 'haʊs]: *Reihenhaus*
343 hub: centre
348 shift: period of work time in a factory, etc.
348 *keema lobia*: minced meat and bean curry
362 demeaning: *erniedrigend*
364 fork out sth. (infml): pay for sth.
366 term sth. as sth.: call sth. sth.
373 frugal ['fru:gl]: using only as much as is necessary
377 appease sb.: make sb. calmer or less angry by giving them what they want

daughter to support, but also his father to appease, who had never forgiven him for leaving home and doing menial jobs in mills in 'Velat.'

The only thing that could win over his father would be the building of a new house, to illustrate his economic well-being and to support his younger brother's family. Three years later, having had enough of textile mills and with his family having joined him, he escaped to the big city of Manchester and started his own manufacturing business. It was a time when knitwear manufacturing was a booming industry in the Northwest and Ardwick had become a manufacturing area. Many Pakistani migrants entered this trade. Samir too purchased an old factory for his knitwear business. It was also a time of social and communal uncertainty. Enoch Powell had done his bit; frightening the host community with his racist speech citing 'the rivers of blood' and leaving the migrants in fear of being thrown out of the country. When the Ugandan refugees started to arrive in the early nineteen seventies after their expulsion by Idi Amin, his friends were very dismal about their own fate in the UK, fearing that they too would be thrown out. For some, the mission or the next urgent goal was to build houses back home to return to if things really got bad in England.

Unlike his friends, Samir had faith in the British justice system and its fairness. He never for one moment believed that something similar could happen in Britain. Unlike some of his friends, his savings went not into a khoti or a villa in Lahore, but in gradually working his way up to a better standard of living for his family, progressing from a terraced house to a detached house in a good area. He concentrated on his children, their education and careers. And the decades simply slipped away, melting away his youth and gradually severing the links with his homeland. His retirement was forced on him; he did not welcome it.

Samir smiled at the young man with the suitcase and turned into the village lane to pay a special call. In the widow's home there was panic as the youngest of the three girls whispered to the others that a man from Velat was standing outside their door. When their mother spotted the foreign visitor, she nearly fainted, but recovered soon enough. Bursting into sobs, she stared at the husband of their benefactor, muttering behind the fold of her long shawl, and gushing the welcome greeting: 'Bismillah! Bismillah!' She owed a lot to this man's wife.

Her three teenage daughters had rushed ahead into their bethak, to make the room presentable. The crocheted edged tablecloth was quickly straightened and dusted, the mirrored beaded cushions on the leather settee hurriedly plumped up and the pair of knitting needles and women's magazine snatched and shoved under the table.

Red-faced and brimming with pleasure, the widow led their very 'special' guest into their humble living room, with the walls lined with their best china propped on wooden sills. It was a quaint sight for him, reminding him of the old days when his father would take him to tour

378 menial job [ˈmiːniəl]: boring or dirty job of low status
388 Enoch Powell [ˌiːnɒk ˈpaʊəl] (1912–1998): right-wing politician, campaigning against foreigners in the UK
391 Ugandan refugees [ˌrefjuˈdʒiːz]: refugees from a country in East-Central Africa fleeing violent conflict and a military dictatorship by Idi Amin402 sever sth. [ˈsevə]: cut sth., end sth. completely
409 faint (v): become unconscious
410 benefactor [ˈbenɪfæktə]: person who gives money or help for a good cause
412 owe sth to sb. [əʊ]: *jdm. etwas schulden, verdanken*
416 settee [seˈtiː]: sofa
419 humble: *bescheiden*

some village for a 'taste of the other life and warm hospitality of the rural people.'

Samir did not know what to say, both touched and embarrassed by their humility and behaviour.

'Please don't bring any refreshments, Cola or Miranda bottles or such – I have a bad stomach,' he glibly lied, saving them the bother and cost of purchasing the bottles from the local village shop. 'I just wanted to see how you all are – and how your daughters are doing – I know my wife always visited you – as she did with the other homes she sponsored …' He stopped, eyes filling up, his Sabiya in front of him.

The widow again burst into loud sobs. 'We are so sorry about your wife's death, she was such a wonderful soul and so good to us! We miss her so much, and she phoned us every month – calling us to the butcher's house to chat with us … always checking that we had enough money for my daughter's expenses and enough grain!'

'Yes – she was a good soul! And we all miss her!' Samir lowered his head to hide his tear-swollen eyes. The widow, touched by his grief, stared in wonder, mouth open, showing her row of uneven top teeth and two missing lower molars. She quickly closed her mouth in embarrassment when he looked up.

Samir looked at the girls shyly staring at him, and could not stop the outburst. His sobbing caused the girls' eyes to fill up. They were used to crying from an early age. Their mother had become a crying machine and often they ended up aping her. Today they found the sight of this older man from England, crying over his wife, very poignant. He was thinking, 'My wife has made a difference to these wretched girls' lives!'

Sobering he wiped his cheeks clean with a tissue proffered shyly by the eldest daughter. As if reading his mind, the widow reminded him, 'Your wife got my oldest daughter married, she helped us with the dowry … here is that daughter … she's visiting us at the moment.' Then her gaze switched to her other daughters. 'Who will now finance these girls' weddings?' Poverty had forced her into straight talking, to unabashedly appeal to the good nature of well-off people like him.

Samir had thought ahead. His pension, even if he did not touch the rest of his savings, would be enough to support this household – an ideal way of honouring his wife and her dying wish. Her last words to all her children and to him had been, 'Do not forget all the families that I've been supporting in my life – earn their heartfelt prayers by helping them. Don't forget to keep my register of widows safe. Don't let anyone die of poverty or ill health! Display your humanity and offer generously your zakat.'

His eyes on the four heads modestly draped with dupattas, Samir meditated on one possible way for these girls to get out of this poverty trap and offered, 'Sister, please educate your daughters … send them to any colleges that you like. I'll pay all their fees and other costs.'

423 rural: in the countryside, not the city
425 humility [hjuːˈmɪləti]: *Demut, Bescheidenheit*
427 glibly: not sincerely
427 bother [ˈbɒðə] (n): trouble
432 sob (n): cry of anguish, sadness
445 ape sb.: copy sb.
446 poignant [ˈpɔɪnjənt]: touching, making you feel sad
447 wretched [ˈretʃɪd]: very unhappy
448 sober (v): *ruhiger werden*
448 proffer sth. (fml): offer sth.
451 dowry [ˈdaʊri]: *Mitgift*
452 gaze (n): look
454 unabashedly [ˌʌnəˈbæʃɪdli]: not shyly or easily embarrassed
454 appeal to sth.: ask for support based on sth.
461 display sth. (v): show sth.

The girls' eyes widened and lit up in wonder. The *Velati* man would do that for them! Go to the town college. The girls' minds were swimming. Their poignant looks and smiling faces cut him to his soul. His own children, including his two daughters, had been educated to the high degree level and had access to great opportunities. Did these poor girls not have a right to the same? He was suddenly struck and dismayed by the inequality of life. How some had everything whilst others simply worried about the next meal!

The youngest girl moved away from the doorway as Samir's village host, who had followed him to the widow's house, entered the room. Catching Samir's eyes, the host signalled to him that dinner was waiting. Samir hastened to add before rising from the settee.

'Don't worry about anything, sister. I'll take care of your financial situation and make sure that you get your remittances on time, including for the wheat. You have our phone numbers, please phone for any extra financial help needed. I'll take care of the furniture for your daughters' dowries just as my Sabiya did for your eldest daughter … I have to go now, and may Allah Pak look after you all!' He felt in his jacket pocket and shyly placed a three-thousand-rupee note in the youngest girl's hand, lowering his gaze in embarrassment in the face of their gratitude.

He politely followed his host out of the small courtyard before turning to look back at the girls shyly peeping out of their door. 'This is their humble world!' he mused, 'And I live in a large house all by myself.' The thought terrified him.

He politely smiled to the other villagers that he passed in the lane. There was no one he recognised and no welcoming look of sudden recognition. And why should there be? He chided himself. He was over seventy years old – and so far he had not seen a soul of that age group in the village.

That night he returned to Lahore to his brother's family. Fear of hospitality had made him flee the village, afraid that if he stayed the night his hosts would incur the cost of breakfast and afternoon dinner the following day. He was familiar with their generosity and excellent hospitality. Already they had spent a lot on his behalf. Until the entire dining table was covered with plates of cakes, pastries, boiled eggs and parathas they would not be happy.

In his brother's home there was no element of guilt – no waiting-upon ceremony. They knew what he liked, and so for breakfast his brother would fetch some warm *kulchas* from the local bakery and the tea would be supplied by his sister-in-law.

Drinking a cool glass of *lassi*, Samir instructed the driver to take him back to Lahore, the city of his birth, the old Mughal capital of India. He wanted to call on the way at the famous Data Gunj Darbar, a favourite shrine of his mother. In his childhood days she eagerly took him to pay

473 dismayed (adj): feeling shocked and disappointed
480 remittance [rɪˈmɪtns] (fml): *Überweisung, Geldsendung*
499 incur costs: *sich Unkosten aufladen*
501 on his behalf: for him
509 Mughal [ˈmuːgɑːl]: old Muslim dynasty of Turkish-Mongolian descent in India
511–512 pay homage to sb. [ˈhɒmɪdʒ, ɒˈmɑːʒ] (fml): worship or offer prayers to sb. to show respect

homage to the saint buried in the tomb, visited by thousands every day from all over the world.

Outside in the Darbar courtyard, the *daig* men were fast at work, serving food from their big pots to the needy and to those keen to take the *tabark*, food offerings, home for their family. When the man distributing bags of pilau rice touched him on his arm, Samir was lost for words and nodded, taking the bag of rice with him inside the building. In the large hall amidst the crowd of male and female devotees, peering through the open windows at the tomb draped with a green and gold embroidered sheet, Samir offered special prayers for his wife's soul, tears gushing out of his eyes. Then a prayer for himself. He repeated the word 'escape' again.

As he sheepishly entered his ancestral home, the mouths of his brother's family fell open. They had not expected him back that night. In fact, they thought he was touring another city and here he was, large as life. Both parties energetically avoided eye contact. His brother's family quickly recovered. They had been lounging around on sofas. It was eight o'clock and the popular drama was about to be telecast. The wife and daughter began panicking. Was their guest fed or did they have to scurry to the kitchen to rustle up a meal for him? Reading their minds perfectly, Samir wryly held the bag of rice in front of him.

'I got my meal from the Darbar, I'm sure it's delicious. Don't worry about me, just carry on watching.' With those words he left them to their drama, before excusing himself. 'I'll go up to my room and have a shower.'

'Yes, please do!' His sister-in-law quickly offered with a toothy grin and orangey *sac*-stained lips, sitting down to enjoy the drama with her daughter.

He came down precisely after nine pm, having given them time to finish watching their serial. In that time, he had showered, eaten the rice from the bag with his fingers and started to gather his belongings. They were expecting him and hurried to greet him, his niece standing up.

'Are you sure you will not want a meal?' his brother asked, not happy at Samir not eating. 'The *Darbar daig* rice was wonderful. Good to eat *tabark* sometimes. It reminds us gently what life is all about – our stomachs. Getting food into our bellies is what we work for, don't we?' His brother cynically nodded, a director of a firm and now retired. He still had two daughters whose marriage and dowries he had to arrange. It was not just the matter of food for him. He envied his brother for having all his children wed and settled. No worries, saving that of having lost a wife.

Aloud he instructed, 'Bano, go and make tea for your uncle!'

A smile fixed on her face, the eldest daughter left for the kitchen, whilst everyone else watched the news.

512 tomb [tu:m]: large grave
519 devotee [ˌdevəˈti:]: *religiöse(r) Verehrer/in, Anhänger/in*
531 rustle up a meal (infml): make a meal quickly

'Tomorrow morning I will check flight times.' Samir slipped in the information whilst sipping his tea. Heads turned, TV forgotten, surprise written on their faces.

'What, brother! Already? You've only been here for just a week!' The sister-in-law rushed to speak.

'I think a week is enough – time to go home!' He replied, a gentle smile peeping across his features as he remembered his daughter Rosie.

Dumbfounded, they stared back at him, but did not challenge or question him further as to why. 'He must be missing his children,' his brother echoed in his head. Once more all heads turned to the programme. As the eldest daughter got up to take the cups back to the kitchen, she smiled at her uncle, asking if he wanted some more tea. He smiled back; it was the first full smile she had accorded him since he had arrived. Then she surprised him and her parents further with her kind offer.

'Uncle please give me your laundry. I will see to it before you leave.'

'You stupid girl! Your uncle is not going yet!' her father chided, red-faced. 'He was only saying it. We are not going to let him go yet.'

His wife quickly echoed the same. 'No, brother, you are not going yet.'

'Don't worry, Bano! I'll get my clothes washed at home,' Samir said, surprising himself. Twice he had used the term 'home.' Was not this his home, the place where he was born?

Chastened and the smile deleted, the eldest daughter took the tray of crockery back to the kitchen. In the lounge her uncle from England had already decided. He stayed up for some more polite talk and then went up to his air-conditioned room. Picking up the remaining items littering the dressing table, he threw them into his suitcase. His love affair with his city of birth was over.

On the plane he found himself sitting next to a man called Ibrahim, of his age group and size; both overweight and uncomfortable with the economy seats and the narrow leg space in front of them. After exchanging polite chitchat they soon got into serious talking and were onto the question as to why they were visiting their country of birth and youth.

'The homeland?' Samir ruminated over the term and shared his musing aloud with his fellow passenger, who had similar home circumstances, including being a widower.

'The one that you have just visited, or the one that you are returning to? The place where you have spent most of your adult life? Which homeland are you trying to escape from?' Samir elaborated, making the man's sun-beaten forehead groove into three deep pleats.

'Escape?' Ibrahim was disconcerted by the term. Samir nonchalantly went on to explain. 'I am escaping back to the UK – and to a new home.'

'New home?'

563 dumbfounded [dʌmˈfaʊndɪd] (adj): surprised, at a loss for words
568 accord sb. sth. [əˈkɔːd] (fml): *jdm. etwas gewähren*
579 chasten sb. [ˈtʃeɪsn]: make sb. feel sorry for sth. they have done
582 air-conditioned: having a system that makes the air colder
587 narrow: having a small distance from one side to the other
591 ruminate over sth. [ˈruːmɪneɪt]: think deeply about sth.
596 elaborate [ɪˈlæbəreɪt] (v): add more information
597 groove into pleats: *sich in Falten legen*
598 disconcerted [ˌdɪskənˈsɜːtɪd] (adj): feeling anxious or confused

'Want to join me?'

The man looked blankly at him, wondering whether this was a joke. Samir chuckling went on to explain.

He returned home not having met the two college friends or walked down the tall nineteenth-century corridors of the Government College of Lahore. Strangely, it really did not matter to him.

Two weeks after his arrival, Samir had moved to an elderly people's home, leaving his five-bedroomed detached house to his four children but keeping his savings and shares to see to the needs of the family he had promised to support. He made a new will, instructing his Solicitor that when he died one of his children would carry on supporting the widow and her daughters. He got his eldest daughter to phone the widow, to reassure her that he had not forgotten his promise. Social and cultural parameters had to be maintained. He was a man and would keep his distance from the widow and not compromise her honour, her *izzat*. They needed his financial help which his wife used to provide; now he would take over her role.

When he spoke to his brother on arrival in Manchester, he was asked when he would return to his homeland. After a pause, Samir asked, 'Homeland? Which homeland? I'm home ...' An awkward silence followed. Then he had added laughing, 'You can visit me next time.'

A week later, the friend he had met on the plane arrived with his daughter, carrying his suitcase. Ibrahim took the room three doors away from Samir's, his gales of laughter echoing down the corridor. Pure joy raced through Samir lifting his spirit as he rushed to show his friend around the home, enthusiastically explaining and reassuring, introducing him to the other house guests he had befriended, Penny and Derrick.

'It's the right decision, my friend. You won't regret it. Wave goodbye to loneliness and heartache ... We are the new English *babus*, living in old people's homes, the ones we used to ridicule once upon a time! Meals on wheels for us now – we have worked so hard – time to enjoy ourselves now, hey!'

From: Asiatic: IIUM Journal of English Language and Literature, *Vol. 3, No. 1, June 2009, ISSN 1985–3106 © Copyright 2009 Asiatic*

602 blankly: in a way that shows no understanding
603 chuckle (v): laugh quietly
609 share (n): *Aktie, Wertpapier*
613 reassure sb. (that ...) [ˌriːəˈʃʊə]: say sth. that makes sb. less worried
614 parameter [pəˈræmɪtə]: (here) rule
630 *babu* [ˈbɑːbuː] (Indian English): rich and powerful person
631 ridicule sb. [ˈrɪdɪkjuːl]: make fun of sb.

Info Qaisra Shahraz

Qaisra Shahraz (born 1958) is a British Pakistani novelist, screenwriter and journalist whose novels and short stories have been translated into many languages. Born in Pakistan, she has lived in Manchester since she was nine. Besides being a successful author, she is also a college inspector, an international teacher trainer and an eductaion consultant. Her work is centred on questions of race, gender and cultural divides, and she is the founder of the Muslim Arts and Culture Festival (MACFEST). Many of her main characters are Muslim women living in Western societies.

Comprehension

2 Tick the correct answer. Only one option is correct.

a Samir …

- **A** rarely visits the Mosque in Longsight.
- **B** never visits the Mosque in Longsight.
- **C** regularly visits the Mosque in Longsight.
- **D** occasionally visits the Mosque in Longsight.

b Samir does not want to go to Manzoor's house because he …

- **A** feels too lonely to see him and his wife together.
- **B** no longer feels welcome there.
- **C** has made other plans.
- **D** feels embarrassed.

c This year Samir and his son Maqbool are celebrating Eid …

- **A** alone.
- **B** at a restaurant.
- **C** in Samir's house with the whole family.
- **D** in Maqbool's house with the whole family.

d The customary family meal is prepared by …

- **A** Samir's wife.
- **B** Maqbool's wife.
- **C** Samir's daughter.
- **D** all the women in the family.

e When Samir announces his plan to go to Pakistan, his children …

- **A** want to join him.
- **B** are completely against his plan.
- **C** are surprised and a bit annoyed.
- **D** are surprised and happy for him.

f When Samir arrives in Lahore, his family there …

- **A** are indifferent.
- **B** react in a hostile way.
- **C** welcome him with open arms.
- **D** welcome him but are a bit shocked.

g Samir did not take up the job offered at the nursing home because …

A he was afraid of the effect the work might have on him.
B he did not like the boss.
C the work was too hard.
D it was not well paid.

h By taking up a job in the textile mill instead, Samir …

A learned a lot.
B thought he made his father proud.
C felt that he had disappointed his father.
D knew that he would not make a lot of money.

i A few years later, as the political situation became more difficult for immigrants, Samir …

A left England for a while.
B left England and never came back.
C nevertheless stayed on in England with his family.
D decided to stay in England but sent his family home again.

j When Samir visits the widow and her daughters, he declines the offer of refreshments because he …

A does not feel thirsty.
B does not want to stay too long.
C is afraid of getting a stomach ache.
D does not want them to spend their money on things for him.

k After Samir has made up his mind to return to England, his brother and the rest of the family …

A do not mind him leaving.
B seem relieved he is going back.
C are unhappy about him leaving.
D try hard to make him stay longer.

3 **a** Work in groups of four or five. Each of you make up three more multiple-choice comprehension questions about the story. Write them on a card and underline the correct answer.
b Mix all the cards. Then take turns in picking a card, reading it out and answering the questions.

4 Collect information about Samir. What is your first impression of him? Make notes here.

____

____

____

____

____

____

____

____

5 Sum up Samir's reasons for going to Pakistan.

6 **a** Describe Samir's initial living conditions and job situation in Blackburn.

b State the different stages of his working life in the UK.

7 Describe the situation of the widow and her daughters as well as their relationship with Sabiya and Samir's family.

Analysis

8 Refer back to your notes in **5**. Did your impression of Samir change while you were reading the rest of the short story? If so, how?

9 Describe how people feel at different moments in the story and explain why. Choose from the adjectives in the box and add more if necessary.

angry · relieved · exhausted · awful · bored · excited · hopeful · happy · unhappy · lonely · lucky · nervous · overjoyed · sad · shocked · embarrassed · shy · sorry · surprised · scared · annoyed · …

10 Explain how the community in Longsight has changed in Samir's view. Think about how different religious houses/buildings signify change.

11 Examine how the author presents the atmosphere at Samir's eldest daughter's house (→ Info box, p. 176).

12 Look back at ll. 208–584. This part of the short story set in Pakistan consists of 7 different sections. Find a suitable heading for each of the sections. The first is done for you as an example.

section	heading
A ll. 208–215	*A not so warm welcome*
B ll. 215–264	
C ll. 265–283	
D ll. 284–337	
E ll. 338–404	
F ll. 405–496	
G ll. 497–523	
H ll. 524–584	

13 Look back at ll. 284–337. Compare Samir and his friend. What makes the friend successful in London? Why isn't Samir?

14 **Writing** Using the perspective of the youngest daughter, rewrite the part of the story when Samir visits the widow and her daughters.

15 Examine how Sabiya is portrayed in the short story.

16 Contrast Samir's life before and after the trip to Pakistan.

Before Samir's trip to Pakistan	After Samir's trip to Pakistan

17 **a** Analyse how the idea of 'home' is presented in the story.
b Compare the idea presented in the story with your own definition of 'home' from **1** (on p. 47).

18 Explain the title of the story.

Beyond the text

19 Evaluate whether in your opinion Samir's decision at the end of the story shows that present-day family structures are failing older people.

20 You choose:

a Speaking Work in pairs. Look back at ll. 120–122 in which Maqbool finds his father. Imagine a short conversation between Maqbool and his wife later that day in which they discuss the situation. Prepare notes and then act out the dialogue.
OR

b Speaking Look back at ll. 232–239. Imagine what Samir would tell his late wife about his decision to go to Pakistan. Prepare notes and then present the monologue.
OR

c Speaking Work in pairs. Look back at ll. 396–401. Imagine a dialogue between Samir and his Pakistani friend in which they discuss if they should build a house in Pakistan or in the UK. Prepare notes and then act out the dialogue.

21 Writing Samir is volunteering as a mentor for an organization that helps young immigrants start a business in Manchester. He has been asked to write a short article for the organization's website in which he uses his own experiences as examples to give advice to eager young entrepreneurs. Write his article.

22 Writing You are taking part in an international project on migration literature. Write an essay commenting on the statement below. Refer to 'The Escape'.

Migrants constantly change their countries of origin and arrival.

B5 'The Rain Missed My Face and Fell Straight to My Shoes' *Saeed Taji Farouky*

Read the short story and complete the tasks on p. 76.

I'm looking for change in my pocket, flicking through the coins all one- and two-pence pieces. I'm trying to make up at least two pounds with all the spare coins because Faris said he can't let me into the theatre any more for free. Otherwise his boss is going to get suspicious and Faris would maybe lose his job so I have to give him some change. I turn over everything I have, which is only eighty-seven pence anyway. He starts counting the coins and I can see it isn't going to be enough. People are behind me in the queue, getting impatient. Faris looks behind him in the booth, then to me, 'It's not even a pound, Samir.'

1 flick through sth.: examine sth. quickly
3 theatre: (here) cinema
4 suspicious [səˈspɪʃəs]: *misstrauisch*

I have to lean down to speak quietly through the gap in the glass, 'I know. I don't have enough. It's OK for now, isn't it?'

'Just go inside, there are other people waiting. I don't have time to argue now.' Faris is scowling, trying not to look me in the eyes. But there's a familiarity we have that means he understands me by now, he knows that I always do this. Faris piles the coins next to the ticket machine and yells for the next person in line.

I used to feel guilty when I tried to get into Faris's theatre for free, but not any more, not since I started letting him on to the tube for nothing – not even one or two pounds. I walk with my ticket into the foyer and look for someone else I recognise. I know it'll either be Youssef or Hamza. Youssef is Egyptian so he gets along well with me. Hamza is I think from Somalia – we don't have much in common; not much. He can't speak English very well, or Arabic, so we can only have very simple conversations about his family. I can tell that Hamza doesn't like me coming in to the cinema, and he's worried about his job as well, but he doesn't know that everyone lets their friends in for free – even the boss and the English people working here. That's why I prefer it when Youssef is at the gate because he knows that there's nothing to worry about.

This time it's Youssef and he smiles and puts out his arms for a hug when he sees me. His hairy arms tickle my neck when he leans in to hug me. He has a thin beard that pricks my face. The other customers in the queue turn to look at us, two men hugging, but Youssef doesn't care. He's a very private man, but somehow he never seems afraid if people notice him. He's never afraid to let people stare at him and wonder who he is. I'm the opposite: I always get anxious when people look at me; I try to make out their reactions to everything I do. I worry they're looking for something that isn't really in me, but if they look hard enough, they might see it anyway. I'm smiling when Youssef hugs me because I haven't seen him in more than two weeks. I'm usually at the cinema every day, sometimes a few times a day.

'Samir! You son of a bitch!'

'Don't swear so loud, people will hear you.' Youssef is hugging me with one hand and tearing tickets with the other. People have to step around us to get through the gate.

'Where were you, I haven't seen you in weeks. Hamza says you haven't been, either.'

'No, I was visiting my Mum, she was sick in hospital. I had to go stay with her in hospital.'

'Your Mum was sick? I didn't know. I'm sorry.' He takes back his arm from around me and steps to the side to tear someone else's ticket. I can see everyone else is getting impatient because he's ignoring them and not telling anyone their screen number. Some people are trying to listen to our conversation. Youssef smiles to his customers as he's talking to me: 'I hope she's OK now, huh?'

13 scowl [skaʊl] (v): look annoyed
14 familiarity [fəˌmɪliˈærəti]: *Vertrautheit*

'No, she died.' Some more people get their tickets torn and walk past us through the gates. We both stand beside each other for a few moments in silence. Customers pass by. Youssef doesn't look at me but puts one hand on my shoulder and is trying to say something sensible while he's tearing the tickets. I finally have to move out of the way to let the other customers through, and his hand falls from my shoulder. I give him a few seconds to think of something to say, but I don't want to make him uncomfortable, with the customers all standing around us, I don't want to embarrass him. 'I'll see you after the film, Youssef …'

'No, I'll see you in there,' he says to me. 'I'm coming in now.' Youssef looks over his shoulder to the far end of the foyer. The toilet door swings open, and I see Hamza clumsily pushing his way out carrying a mop in one hand and bucket in the other. Youssef tries to wave him over, but Hamza doesn't see him. He's just finished the day's third cleaning, mopping up all the shit and piss and disgusting things people leave behind in cheap toilets when they don't care about them. I used to do that job as well, anyone who works in the cinema has to do all the jobs – except Hamza who doesn't sell or tear tickets because of his English. When he sees Youssef waving, he carefully puts the mop and bucket into the service closet and walks over. His dark black skin shines blue under the halogen lights of the foyer, thin arms pressed tightly to his sides and hands forced into his pockets. Youssef asks Hamza to tear the tickets in his place, and Hamza says OK because Youssef has a personality that makes people want to do what he says. He doesn't push, but he always manages to convince you that his ideas are clever or sensible. While I was working there, he always got me to count the money at the end of the night, which was the worst job, and no one wanted to do it because it was so boring and you were always the last to leave. He also managed to convince me, every Friday night, to take a few pounds from the till and go drinking with him. I never wanted to steal and I didn't drink before I worked there but Youssef made me want to do all of that.

He takes my arm and walks me through the swinging doors and into one of the theatres, looking for spaces at the back right, under the balcony. That's where you always find the people who got in for free or people who just snuck in or people who paid for one ticket in the morning and stayed in the cinema all day moving from film to film, sometimes sleeping behind the seats if no one saw them. Youssef and I take the empty seats behind two boys I recognise, two boys that I always see here. They sit next to each other and pass a mobile phone between them, sometimes both talking on it, sometimes just writing messages. Next to us, there's one Arab or Iranian man who is a bit older than me and has a beard and looks like a religious man, but I always see him drinking cans of beer in his seat. He's sitting next to the air conditioner vent. I see one black guy who once brought a prostitute in, or maybe not a prostitute but a girl who didn't mind doing things in a

58 sensible [ˈsensəbl]: *vernünftig*
66 clumsy: *ungeschickt*
75 halogen [ˈhælədʒən]
84 till (n): cash box
89 sneak in (snuck, snuck): enter without being seen
97–98 air conditioner vent: *Lüftungsöffnung der Klimaanlage*

cinema and that's what they did. I also see a fat white man who usually sits a few rows ahead and at the end of the film always asks Youssef and me and anyone else I'm with, 'What did you boys think of that?' Especially when it's a film about war: 'What did you boys think of that?' with his arms waving and the loose skin billowing. There are some other people around but I don't recognise them. Everyone else, the real customers, are sitting further up so they can see the screen. Back here no one cares if we talk because they're not here to see the film anyway, so Youssef and I talk and he asks me what happened to my mother and I tell him.

I tell him that she was in Cairo when she got sick and they wanted her to go to hospital there, but no one could pay for it. So they thought she could get treated in London for free, but of course they had to pay for the plane ticket and still no one had the money. My family tried to put everything they had together but it still wasn't enough, and at the same time my cousin was having a baby so they needed that money. That's when I stole the whole day's till from the cinema, and with that I bought the plane ticket. The next day I lost my job. All this Youssef knew. But since my Mum made it to London, that was seventeen days ago, I hadn't seen him or been to the cinema at all. I was staying with my Mum in hospital. At midnight I would go to work in the underground stations until 8 a.m., then I could go back to the hospital.

'After seventeen days she died. It was very slow. And I have to spend all my money again to send her body back to Cairo. I can't even go with her. I have to look for another job.' I'm trying to raise my voice above the sounds of the screaming coming from the film. It's a film about a woman who finds out her daughter is being followed by a killer, that's what I understand so far, and the woman now is trying to find out who the killer is and what he wants with her daughter. Youssef says in Arabic the things that we will always say when someone dies, that is, 'She will live on inside you,' and 'God have mercy on you,' and 'God give you good health.' These things we never really have to think about because they are phrases already written by generations and hundreds of years of people's parents dying. Generations of killing children and starving and being murdered in the name of God. We can recite the phrases and then forget about the death and move on. I know Youssef won't forget, but it always sounds shallow when someone uses these phrases. And the person grieving knows those words all sound empty and insincere but there's nothing anyone can do about it. We keep using them.

The killer turns out to be someone the mother knows and now she's chasing him across the city. There's a policeman with her, and the policeman's father was shot before when he was also a policeman.

'Samir, I know someone who can do it properly here, who can do a Muslim funeral here.'

104 billow (v): move like cloth in the wind
112 get treated for free: refers to the NHS (National Health Service) of the UK, where emergency services are available to everyone at no cost, regardless of citizenship
116 the whole day's till: *die Tageseinnahmen*
136 shallow: *hohl*
137 grieve: *trauern*
137 insincere [ˌɪnsɪnˈsɪə]: *unaufrichtig*

'No, she's supposed to be buried in Cairo. Everyone there is waiting for me to send her but I don't have the money. I need money.' It reminds me of when I would break something in my grandmother's house. The place was filled with antiques and whenever we went to visit, when I was younger, I would always break something. She would tell me it was all right as long as I paid for it, and I would say 'Later,' but I never did pay for anything.

'I don't have anything I can give you.' Youssef is talking to me but looking straight ahead, his eyes on the screen.

'I wasn't expecting anything from you.' I turn my head to face him. 'That's not what I meant. I just wanted to tell you.' Now the woman and the policeman find the killer just before he reaches the daughter. The daughter doesn't know he's after her. The policeman gets shot and dies before the killer falls from the roof or from a balcony. The lights come up and everyone slides from out of their chairs and throws empty boxes and cups on the floor and the fat white man sees us and his eyes get wide. 'Well, what did you boys think of *that*?' He crosses his arms over his belly and looks at both of us with relish, waiting for a reply, but I'm not going to say anything. Youssef finally offers this: 'I think the girl was stupid, she should have known he was coming to kill her!' The fat man nods his head, 'I was thinking that as well,' and smiles broadly to himself as he limps out of the cinema with the other customers.

When I stole the money from the cinema, everyone else said they wouldn't tell the boss it was me. They knew it was me because I'd been talking about it for a few days, but all of us working there stayed together and usually let the rest of the staff get away with whatever they were doing. No one wants to cause any problems for themselves, and the best way to avoid that is to do your job. Don't say anything if you aren't asked. We're all illegal so no point in bringing trouble on all of us. They said they wouldn't tell the boss who it was but everyone knew and someone must have said something in the end because the boss told me straight, the next morning, that I didn't have a job there any more. But that didn't bother me, because I had already taken the money the night before and hidden it in my flat. Now I think it would have been better if I had just taken the money for myself. Just kept it. My mother died anyway, better for her to have died in Cairo with the family and then be buried there straight away. I say that to Youssef but he tries to make me feel better and says, 'There was no way to know, was there? You couldn't have known. You did what you could.' Now I have to go through losing her and losing all the money at the same time.

As Youssef and I walk out of the cinema, Hamza follows to tell us something. He's trying to give us a message, but he's difficult to understand because of his English. Youssef and I eventually figure out that the message has to do with the boss; he says I can't come to the cinema any more since I lost my job. If he sees me here again he'll call

161 belly (infml): *Bauch*
161 relish ['relɪʃ] (n): enjoyment
165 limp (v): walk unsteadily

the police and have me arrested. Youssef laughs because he laughs when he's nervous. My face is straight, I don't have the energy to react. When Hamza says the word 'police', I imagine the policeman from the film. I imagine him chasing me in a taxi and getting shot before I fall off a roof. Now I'll have to find somewhere else to waste hours of every day. Somewhere else dark to hide in when I can't bear to go back to the flat and I can't afford a proper meal. I'll have to find somewhere else to buy my hashish from.

The next night I meet Youssef outside the cinema when he's done working, and he brings Aqil with him, a friend from Iraq. Aqil was in the army there but he thought because he had a doctorate degree in physics he shouldn't be in the army. So the government said he could work on their physics programme, but he escaped to come to England instead. Aqil is short and very wide, now he wears thick glasses and has his hair combed over the top. When he was younger he was very handsome – he showed me a picture of himself when he was a weight-lifter. He also used to be on the National Weight-Lifting Team, then he came to London and started working in a video shop. He watches the news all day on the shop's television even though he's supposed to play the new films.

We walk to a café not far from the cinema, on one of the smaller streets behind Charing Cross Road. There's a Turkish guy who runs the place, they sell fish and chips and pies. Aqil sits facing me and looks into his cup of coffee for a few minutes before starting with, 'Samir, can you believe Blair? He is such a fool! I'm serious, he is a fool if he thinks he can control Iraq like this: Be democratic …' he lays down his coffee and holds his two hands up as though he's aiming a rifle at my chest '… or I'll kill you. This is his foreign policy.' I look down at his fingers pointed to my chest. That's how our conversations always begin, then we go on from there insulting European and American leaders. At some point in every conversation Aqil will say, 'And don't forget, it's really our fault. We let them push us around like this …' and no one's satisfied by the end of it. I once saw Aqil crying when they were showing on TV pictures of people in Iraq, men on the streets of Baghdad, stealing things from the National Museum and smashing everything to pieces. The city and the windows and someone's car and banks and people's houses, all being taken to bits. 'Those statues', he said, pointing to images of stolen antiques on the screen, 'were made when Europeans were still running around in the mud! Living in caves!'

I drink my third coffee and Aqil asks about my mother. He must have heard from someone else that she was sick. I don't say anything, but Youssef shakes his head and waves a finger at Aqil. We talk about marriage instead. I've been thinking about it for months now, but I haven't met anyone I love. We decide maybe I don't have to wait to find someone I love. Then on the TV there are pictures of piles of dead bodies

199 doctorate degree [ˈdɒktərət]: *Doktor(titel), Promotion*
204 handsome [ˈhænsəm]: attractive
213 Blair = Tony Blair, British Prime Minister (1997–2007)

but I can't tell if they're American or Iraqi. We've been sitting in the café for two and a half hours by now, waiting for our night shifts to start. I can see girls walking past outside – girls dressed up to go out with their friends, girls in suits on their way back from work (maybe they have to work late or they're sleeping with the boss), girls already drunk, girls who look scared to walk in the streets alone, girls who look really ill and they're trying to find someone to pay them for sex. While looking out the door, looking at the girls passing, I ask Aqil if he knows where I can get some money. I carefully ask, 'What about you, do you have any money I can borrow?' He has his fingers locked together, resting on the tablet and he opens his hands to answer with enthusiasm, 'If I knew where to get money, I would get it!' and Youssef and I laugh with him. It's pathetic and we know it's true but we laugh with him. Everyone is always looking for ways to make money. I once went round to people in the streets with a stolen stereo and tried to persuade someone to buy it, but no one would even talk to me. I didn't steal it but the man who stole it asked me to sell it for him and said I could keep some of the money. I hated to think of myself as a criminal. I thought if I stayed far away from the guy who stole it, if I didn't get close to him, I would be fine. I mean, I would still be clean. But it didn't work and I couldn't sell the stereo and I still felt like a thief. That made me sick. Aqil would often say about himself, 'I left my country to escape from criminals and I came here, and I became a criminal!' That's how I felt with the stereo. But Aqil reads a lot and watches the news all day so he always thinks too much about what he's going through. Youssef and I try not to think about it; we go to the cinema and watch films instead.

Aqil comes in to see me one night when I'm working in the kitchen of Café Tangier. I got the job from someone Youssef knows who used to be in the military in Egypt. His father was something like a captain under King Farouk and he had to leave the country with the king during the revolution. Youssef's friend got me a job serving tables at the Tangier and that was good money. Sometimes I could overcharge tourists, or foreigners who had just arrived in London, by one or two pounds and they wouldn't notice because they couldn't read the menu. But I can't serve in the restaurant any more after the police came and found me and some Hungarian girls working without papers. So I moved to the kitchen. I can still work in the kitchen and probably no one will find me there. That's what I mean by feeling like a criminal. I'm not doing anything illegal, I'm only trying to make a living. Washing up in a kitchen, my family wouldn't believe it. That would be a disgrace. That's why I don't tell them what I'm doing. I tell them instead that I'm doing fine and I'm happy and making money. I can't tell them I came to London to become a criminal. When I look at myself, I don't see a criminal. I don't see a good man. All I want is to live simply. I don't want to get rich, suck the money out of this country. No one would believe that,

235 night shift: *Nachtschicht*
246 pathetic [pəˈθetɪk] (infml): sad
263 King Farouk = Farouk I: King of Egypt (1936–1952)
265 overcharge sb.: take more money than allowed from sb.
273 disgrace: *Schande*

they don't imagine that at all. I want to tell them, 'I'm only trying to earn a living. You have to work too – I'm just working.' That's what it's like in the kitchen.

Aqil comes by to tell me there's a car coming in from France. His cousin is coming to London for the weekend to meet him and pick up a few days of building work around Holland Park. There are a lot of rich Arabs in Holland Park who pay to have work done. Some of them prefer to have other Arabs working for them. Some people say it's because they want to give back to the poorer ones in London, to show their appreciation, but I think it's because they want to be reminded of what things were like for them at home, when they had servants and maids.

'We can go with them to Paris. It's my cousin who moved to Syria, he speaks French.'

'What would we do there?'

'We could find something else there. My brother can help us find work.'

'What kind of work?'

'I don't know. He says it's better than here.'

But I don't speak French. I don't know Paris at all. By now I'm used to where things are in London: where the money is, where there are jobs going and which ones are safe. That takes a lot of time to learn, I stand over the sink, with Aqil next to me hovering like he's waiting for an answer right now. He's sitting on the counter and his legs don't touch the floor. I stop washing and hold my hands down to let some of the soap drip from my fingers. My shirt was white, now it's grey, spattered with water from the sink. I'm thinking about Paris and what it must look like at night compared to London, whether it also has a Soho with mini-cabs and empty beer cans and girls who look sick and counting the money in the till until midnight. And mothers coming over because they have no money and dying in the city.

I hear Aqil's voice mumbling, but I don't hear the words clearly. I look over and see his lips moving with the same sound but I don't hear his voice. I hear the words to an old song, one where the diva sings, 'The world is a cigarette and a drink, when people abandon you …' and her voice moans with the floating sound of the strings. Most people would say she means the cigarette and the drink are all you have left. But I always thought she was saying that everywhere you can see chances. Everywhere you see little insignificant things that can comfort you. Maybe it's a drink or a cigarette or a girl but when everything is lost, you find suddenly there are little pieces everywhere that give you hope, more hope than when things were going well. You can see hope in everything. This is what I'm hearing until Aqil jumps down from the counter and brushes his hands on his trousers. He starts to look apologetic as he turns to walk out of the kitchen. He pauses before the door to say, 'Youssef is coming with me,' and that's the sound of the orchestra rising in a crescendo. I know I'll be alone if I decide not to go

288 appreciation [əˌpriːʃiˈeɪʃn]: *Wertschätzung*
304 Soho: district of London
312 moan (v): make a low sound
315 insignificant [ˌɪnsɪɡˈnɪfɪkənt]: unimportant

with them. I couldn't stand being alone. I turn to face Aqil and he can see on my face what I'm thinking: that I'm afraid to be alone. That I'm afraid to go to Paris. This is like everything else that controls me.

I leave the restaurant early. There aren't many customers anyway so I'll finish washing in the morning. I stand in the doorway and I see the rain hitting the pavement in some spots where it's lit orange by the street lamps. I remember then that I still have a hole in my left shoe, where the sole is split, and if I walk out like this the water's going to soak through my sock and get my foot wet. I'm feeling sick now, sick in my stomach like I'm hungry or I have a hangover but I can't get rid of the sensation. Even when I eat something. I'm just sick thinking of what Aqil mentioned. The idea of going to Paris. I buy four cans of cheap beer from the newsagent's and I open the first one just as I'm stepping on to the tube to get me out of Stoke Newington and all the way down to south London where I can hide behind the warehouses and factories. My foot is already soaking wet. I wish I could have done something like the man who escaped from Egypt with King Farouk. I could be running from something dangerous – that would be honourable. But I'm just running around looking for spare jobs and trying to avoid the police. If I was in exile with the king, no one would look at me like I was a criminal. I could say, 'I did it for my country,' or, 'I did it for my king,' and it would be glorious. English people would understand that's something you have to do, to save your king, and that would be a good reason to be on the run or to be afraid all the time. That would be a good reason to hide my money and buy four cans of beer every once in a while and drink them on my own. Or a good reason to bring your mother over and watch her die, because that's how people in exile have to live. My family could be angry at me but they couldn't be ashamed of me because everyone would know I did it for my country first, and I was willing to die for my country. But I didn't die and I escaped to London. That's my fantasy.

I'm still feeling sick on the tube, and people are watching me now drinking my beer and still wearing my dirty clothes from work. In front of me is a girl sleeping with her head resting on the glass. I can still see the oil from other people's hair smeared on the glass but the girl doesn't seem to notice. She's very young, the girl, and starting to look pretty. I scratch my back through my shirt. Then I have to reach under my shirt to scratch the skin properly, with my nails. The girl opens her eyes while I'm still looking at her, but I forget to smile. She quickly shuts her eyes again, pretending to sleep. I don't know what else to say to her, except, 'I had to escape from the revolution. They were going to kill me if I didn't escape, because I wanted to save my king. Because I love my king.' I only say that because I'm a little drunk by now. Otherwise it's just my own fantasy.

From: Maggie Hamand (publisher): Underwords: The Hidden City.
London: Maia Press, 2005, pp. 85–100

332 soak through sth. (v): make sth. very wet
338 warehouse: *Lagerhalle*
341 honourable [ˈɒnərəbl]: *ehrenhaft*
345 glorious: very great

Info Saeed Taji Farouky

Saeed Taji Farouky is a Palestinian photographer and film-maker best known for his documentary films *The Runner* (2013), *Tell Spring Not to Come This Year* (2015) and *Strange Cities Are Familiar* (2018). He has lived most of his life in the UK. His film projects are usually based in Muslim countries of North Africa and Asia.

Info Egypt, the Suez Canal and the UK

The construction of the Suez Canal (1856–1869) by a French consortium thrust Egypt into the focus of European politics. Britain had opposed construction, as the canal – which links the Mediterranean and the Red Sea – threatened British interests. Before construction, the often dangerous sea route for goods travelling between Europe and Asia was almost completely in British hands. The Suez Canal shortened the distance by thousands of kilometres.
The canal initially belonged jointly to France and Egypt. When debt forced the Khedive (viceroy) of Egypt to sell his share of 44 % in 1875, the government of the UK stepped in. In 1882, British troops were sent to the Canal Zone to repress a local rebellion. Since then, while the Suez Canal officially belonged to Egypt, it was effectively under British control and played a major role in the further colonization of Africa.
In 1952, Egyptian officers rebelled against the King of Egypt, Farouk I, forcing him into exile in Italy and establishing a military dictatorship. The new leaders took control of the Suez Canal. In 1956, the UK made an abortive attempt to regain military control of the canal, but opposition from Canada and the United States forced them to back down. The incident, known as the Suez Crisis, is sometimes pointed to as the beginning of the end of the UK as a world power.

Farouk I, King of Egypt (1936–1952)

Info Tony Blair and the Iraq War (2003–2011)

Tensions mounted in 2002 as US President George W. Bush (2001–2009) repeatedly accused Iraqi ruler Saddam Hussein of supporting terrorism and of possessing weapons of mass destruction. Although UN investigations found no evidence that Iraq had violated international law, Bush launched a military invasion in March 2003, leading to a speedy collapse of the Iraqi government. US forces were supported mainly by the British, who played a major role in the occupation of Iraq. France, Germany and Russia maintained that there was no justification for an invasion and refused to get involved. In fact, no weapons of mass destruction were discovered in Iraq. British Prime Minister Tony Blair (1997–2007) came under attack in the UK for his uncritical support of Bush. The removal of Saddam and his clan by foreign powers led to a period of sectarian conflict between rival groups that continues to the present day.

Comprehension

1 Describe Samir's situation as presented in the story.

Analysis

2 Examine the way the story is told and the effect this has on the reader (→ Info box, p. 29).
3 Examine the role that romantic fantasies and popular culture play in the story. How do they influence Samir's thinking?
4 Describe the impression Samir makes on the reader. Refer to examples from the story.

Beyond the text

5 Assess the title of the story.
6 a **Viewing** Watch the video about Najem Al Khalaf, a Syrian refugee living in Hanover, Germany.

Video online:
cornelsen.de
Code: yarobo

b While you watch the video a second time, answer the following questions:

A Why does Najem report on the opening of a supermarket? ____________________

____

B Why did he leave his home country? ____________________

____

C How did he come to Germany? ____________________

____

D What has he done to adapt to life in Germany? ____________________

____

E What is he doing at present? ____________________

____

F What does 'arriving' mean to him? ____________________

____

c Compare Najem with Samir from the short story.

B6 Return Home *Mfoniso Udofia*

Read the play and complete the tasks on p. 84.

Sunset hours. May 2020. Mojave Desert in upper Arizona. Grace, a pristine trailer, sits on the outskirts of the desert scene, huge, hulking and out of place. Grace's passengers, two women named Deidre and Fatima, lounge on a blanket that has been thrown over a worn-down boulder. The landscape is comprised of a thousand shades of brown and tan and, every now and then, tough verdant green breaks up the palette. These women, Deidre and Fatima, African American and Somali respectively, have been sitting on the boulder, in quiet, for quite a long while, looking at the horizon.

1 Mojave Desert [məʊˌhɑːvi ˈdezət]: large desert located mainly in Southern California, but also in Nevada, Arizona and Utah
2 pristine [ˈprɪstiːn]: clean and new-looking
2 trailer (AE) = mobile home, caravan (BE)
2 outskirts (pl): parts of a city that are further from the centre
2 hulking (adj): very big and heavy
3 Deidre [ˈdɪədri]
4 lounge (v): relax
5 boulder: large rock
5 be comprised of sth. (fml): be made up of sth.
6 verdant green [ˈvɜːdnt]: colour of fresh grass
8 respectively: *beziehungsweise*
15 dead winter (infml): middle of winter
15 10 degrees = 10° F(ahrenheit) (= −12° C)

Deidre *(breaking the silence)***:** We have been coming over here since we were –

Fatima: Too young.

Deidre: Yea. You always loved this place.

Fatima: Mm-hm.

Deidre: It could be dead winter. 10 degrees on a good day and you'd still want to camp out.

Fatima: It was the only place my parents liked.
…
No one was here. I couldn't get into trouble. And you and I were young. I think I could have walked here … they would have let me, and by myself too. Maybe without even asking permission.

Deidre: I doubt that.

Fatima: You're right. Probably not. But it felt like – like heaven. Haven heaven. Heaven haven. It broke all the rules.

...

You liked it too, right? I never asked you for real if –

Deidre: I mean. I liked it – I like it. It's alright. I just liked coming here cause you liked coming here and. It's sorta dry and. It's kind of – I don't know – sparse and. Fatima. It's hot. Can we go back in the trailer, please?

Fatima: You call this hot? You all have no idea of hot. This is a cool day. Breezy! The air is fresh and light and –

Deidre: Yea. No. It's pretty fucking hot.

Fatima: Wimp.

Deidre: This wimp needs a drink. Can we –

Fatima: 10 minutes. No – 15 minutes. Just sit with me for 15 minutes. Before the girls come.

They sit in silence. Looking over the Arizona desert.

Fatima: Look. Look, look look. See that bush? It looks like it was eaten by fire.

Deidre: Everything here looks like it was burnt up in a fire. Everything probably was. Tima. For god's sake. I'm baking –

Fatima: And look at that stump.

Deidre: It's a freaking stump.

Fatima: Why are you so tense? Relax. Look around you. It's beautiful.

24 haven ['heɪvn]: place where you feel safe
27 for real (infml): seriously
29 cause (infml): because
29 sorta (infml): sort of
30 sparse: present in small numbers
35 wimp (derog, sl): weak person 45 stump: *Baumstumpf*
45 freaking (AE, sl): word used to add emphasis, often negative
46 tense (adj): not relaxed

The Mojave Desert

Deidre: I'm not – I'm not tense. I'm – I'm just. You know what? You can stay here. Enjoy the stumps and some heat stroke, I don't know. I should make myself a drink and – or –

Fatima: Of all the places I have seen, I prefer this one. The sand and the – This country has a little bit of everything.

Deidre: I got cooler and some tonic water for some mixed drinks. The ladies like it fruity but I know you got a taste for gin and quinine. So why don't we –

Fatima: Dee.

Deidre *(sharply)***:** What?
…
Hey. You know, you called me here. You asked me to drive us out here. Now you are sitting on this hot-ass rock looking at the desert like you're never gonna see it again. Cause you probably aren't ever gonna –

Fatima: I know what I did. I know what I asked from you. And you came. Thank you. I just want 15 minutes. Before the other girls come and we start a new thing. You and me. Before the party starts. You used to want to sit with me.

They sit in silence.

Deidre *(cutting through the silence)***:** … So you are scared?

Fatima: About what?

Deidre: Fatima.

Fatima: What?

Deidre: I have never known you to be so …

Fatima: So what?

Deidre: Ha! OK.
…
So cagey.

Fatima: Am I scared about what? Speak plain.

Deidre: In the next few weeks, Fatima Ibrahim becomes Fatima Suleiman.

Fatima: Hm.

Deidre: Come on. Tell me about him. I don't know a thing.

Fatima: Oh – OK. You don't want a drink. You don't wanna enjoy out here, with me. You wanna talk about –

49 heat stroke: *Hitzeschlag*
53 cooler (n): (here) alcoholic drink
55 quinine: bitter ingredient found in tonic water
56 Dee: short for Deidre
61 gonna (infml): going to **77** cagey (infml): unwilling to speak openly
82 wanna (infml): want to

Deidre: Yea.

Fatima: He is, according to my father, a very important man. He did finance here in America and he has businesses back in Somalia. I don't know how many. But. More than one and –

Deidre: Cool. Cool, a rich guy! … That's great! Didn't know that but, cool.
So …
So, if he has businesses back there you'll be there too.
You'll have to go back? Like, whenever he goes back.

Fatima: Of course.

Deidre: Yea.
…
Have you met him?

Fatima: I have seen him. Twice now. He is not bad- looking. He is, kind of charming actually –

Deidre: Cool!

Fatima: He also does business in America.
It's not like I will be gone forever.

Deidre: Girl. I get it. He's a businessman. It's a good marriage match. You broke it all down to me when we were like – what 15? 15 or so you told me. Remember?

Fatima: Yea.

Silence.

Fatima: You know, a lot is changing. We have women running in the Olympics and –

Deidre *(matter-of-factly)***:** One of them is a dual citizen and the other couldn't train in any sporting institutions or publicly. And. We are talking about Somalia, not Kuwait. Things are a little different in Somalia.

Fatima: Since when do you read the papers?

Deidre: Since I was 15.

Silence.

Fatima: Dee, nothing too much will change. Whenever I am back in the AZ, I will call you and we can meet here and drink gins and wines and smoke and –

Deidre: You don't fit in there anymore. It's not going to work –

85 according to my father: in my father's opinion
109 dual citizen: person who has two nationalities
117 the AZ [ˌeɪ ˈziː] (AE, sl): Arizona

Fatima: I called you to meet me before everyone else because I wanted to see you before I –

Deidre: You wear jeans over here. I like your jeans. And I like your hair. And I like –

Fatima: I can wear most anything under my wrappers. It is my hair, not yours. I will be fine. You will be fine.

Deidre: I thought that –
You know when you first came here and we were little. You would tell me things, these terrible stories about – Don't you even care about your own choice? I mean, you could have said no. Your father – your father is – you haven't broken your back for your father since you were *(gesturing)* this freaking high. And if 'no' didn't work then you could've run. I would have taken you in. You didn't tell me about Amir until a week ago. I have seen you, Tima. We went shopping last week and I had no idea until Thursday … no idea about a wedding to a Somalian businessman arranged by your –

Fatima: I didn't want to say anything.

Deidre: You are getting married to a man who –

Fatima: I want to sit outside with my best friend, Dee, in peace for 15 – no, what is now 10 minutes, before the rest of our other friends come to give me a pre-wedding wedding party. Before other people got here I wanted to spend time with you. What a strong choice.
My choice.

Deidre: There are other choices you could have made.
Still can make –

Fatima: I told you in high school. I told you everything you needed to know about me. I am at peace with Somalia, Dee. I fight her when I fight her and I love her all the way that I love her. You can stand in solidarity with me, or criticize the decisions I make.

Deidre: But you didn't make them. Your dad did.

Fatima: OK. But – that's my home. I am going back, Amir is nice, I can learn to love him, love him. Not all arranged marriages end in strife. I am just as much a woman there as I am here.

Deidre: No! You're not. I remember when we were younger and you would tell me –

Fatima: I am no longer younger, Dee.

124 wrapper (West African English): loose clothing worn by women in some West African countries
130–131 break your back (for sb.) (sl): make a lot of effort (to please sb.)
131 gesture ['dʒestʃə] (v): make a movement in order to communicate
155 strife (n, fml): conflict

Deidre: You don't have the choice whether you can come see me. Whether I can come see you. Can I even go and see you?

Fatima: I don't know.

Deidre: The way women are over there is uncivilized! Every rule is made up by men.
Everything!

Fatima *(sharply)*: What about here?!
...
I know you love me, but this way that you love me ...
I can't accept it.
...
Dee. You wear your hair out, and wear jeans and do all these things Muslim women do not. This freedom you all have is ... is –
How glorious must you feel hiding behind your makeup and your fingernails and your hair weave? How powerful are you when you hit the glass ceilings? How Amazonian are you, breaking your back in heels and killing yourself with Spanx. Smiling really wide instead of yelling and pretending that you are equal when statistics show that you are not. I have done it. I fought my father to do it. I know what 'freedom' is. I can mouth off and pretend like I am not invisible, while the world here in America is still run by men. I did it. For 20 some odd years. What is the difference? And yes, Somalia is not here and America has more illusion of freedom but I am a woman wherever I am. And I am strong enough to keep my body and heart safe. I have done it. I was not forced. The proposition of a husband was made and I listened and I thought and I met him and I ... I said yes. Me. I said yes. Right or wrong. I said yes to my father. And I am going home. My home. I grew up there. I am –

Deidre: You're missing my point.

Fatima: You're missing mine.

Deidre: It's not that simple.

Fatima: Dee, stop trying to fix me and sit next to me. I am not a project. And, when I need help, you will be there listening for me. Right? As a friend. I love you beyond. And for the 100th time. I want special moments with you just before I become Suleiman. We now have five minutes. If that. Sit with me before people come to celebrate my going home.

170 wear your hair out: wear your hair uncovered
173 glorious: very beautiful
173 makeup (AE) = make-up (BE)
174 hair weave: hair extension
175 glass ceiling: unfair attitudes that keep women from getting better opportunities
175 Amazonian (adj): (here) like an Amazon, a female warrior in Greek mythology
176 heels (pl, infml): high-heeled shoes
176 Spanx: brand of body-shaping underwear for women
177 yell (v, infml): shout
180 mouth off (infml): say your opinion loudly
181–182 20 some odd years: about 20 years
186 proposition: suggestion
190 miss the point (infml): not understand what sb. is trying to say

Deidre: I don't think you're right. I think you're wrong. I think you're thinking with the soft part of you.

Fatima: Because I am deciding something differently, doesn't make me less than you.

Deidre: I don't know. All I know is – I am going to miss you.

Fatima: I know. It's why I am carving out time. And, I will always carve out time. I will find you.

Silence.

Deidre: It kind of does look like that bush was burnt.

Fatima: Hm. Yes. It is beautiful.

Deidre: And the sun is like –

Fatima: Fire.

Deidre: We should see if there are those hollowed-out rocks that used to –

Fatima: Yes!

Deidre: You'll find me if you need me?

Fatima: Of course. And if you need me, it is old-fashioned, but post still works.

From: Return Home*, 2017. Published by permission of The Gersh Agency*

204 carve out time: *sich Zeit nehmen*
211 hollowed(-out): having a hole or empty space inside

Info Mfoniso Udofia

Mfoniso Udofia is a Nigerian-American actor, producer, playwright and writer. Her parents emigrated to the USA in the 1970s. Udofia grew up trying to reconcile her American upbringing and her Nigerian heritage, which inspired her to write her first play *The Grove*. She had so much to say on the topics of immigration, conflicting identities and the stereotypes that people have about immigrants and their descendants that the play became a 9-play cycle called *The Ufot Cycle*. Udofia is also a television writer, having worked on Netflix's *13 Reasons Why* as well as *Little America* and *Pachinko*. She has also appeared as an actress in Ngozi Anyanwu's off-Broadway play *The Homecoming Queen* and the feature film *Fred Won't Move Out*.

Comprehension

1 a Speaking **Hot Seat:** One person sits in front of the group and takes the role of Deidre. The others ask her questions. (Deidre can choose not to answer.) After the third question, Deidre chooses a new person to play her role.

b Speaking Do the same for Fatima.

2 a Actors sometimes prepare their role by writing so-called subtexts, in which they express what is going through their character's mind while they speak the dialogue. Together with a partner, choose one of the following quotes from the play (both of you must choose the same quote). Then write (separately) subtexts in which you say what you think your character really means with her words. Examine the context of the quote before you begin.

A Deidre: I mean. I liked it – I like it. It's alright. I just liked coming here cause you liked coming here and. It's sorta dry and. It's kind of – I don't know – sparse and. Fatima. It's hot. Can we go back in the trailer, please? (ll. 28–31)

From: Mfoniso Udofia: Return Home*, 2017. Unpublished manuscript, The Gersh Agency, p. 3*

B Fatima: I can wear most anything under my wrappers. It is my hair, not yours. I will be fine. You will be fine. (ll. 124–125)

From: Mfoniso Udofia: Return Home*, 2017. Unpublished manuscript, The Gersh Agency, p. 6*

b Compare your subtexts and discuss the points on which you differ.

c Swap subtexts with students who have chosen the other quote. Read and compare what they have written.

Analysis

3 Use the 'silences' in the play to divide the dialogue into sections. Examine how the relationship between the two characters develops from one section to the next.

4 Explain why Fatima's decision to marry a man her father has chosen for her leads to a conflict with Deidre.

Beyond the text

5 Discuss the different ideas of freedom presented in the play, in particular how they affect the status of women in society.

6 Using Fatima as an example, write a text on the opportunities and dilemmas of living in two different societies.

Part C
Post-reading activities

C1 Mediation: The meaning of *migration*

Ein einführendes Soziologie-Buch für Studierende erklärt den Begriff *Migration* wie folgt:

Migration bezeichnet eine dauerhafte Verlagerung des Wohnortes, wobei unter Migration sowohl Wanderungen über Staatsgrenzen hinweg *(Immigration und Emigration)* als auch innerhalb staatlicher Grenzen *(Binnenmigration)* verstanden werden. Nicht darunter fallen Urlaubsreisen oder andere kurzfristige Formen. Hingegen kann sich der Begriff sowohl auf freiwillige wie auf unfreiwillige (Flucht, Vertreibung) Migration beziehen. Diese begrifflichen Unterscheidungen sind nützlich, die Realität jedoch komplizierter.

Eine überkommene Auffassung versteht Migration als einmaligen Vorgang, als Umzug von einem Ort zu einem anderen, der mit der Lösung aus einem sozialen Kontext und dem Niederlassen und Einfügen in ein neues soziales Umfeld verbunden ist. Schon lange hat sich aber gezeigt, dass diese Vorstellung zu naiv ist. In der Realität finden sich immer mehr Mischformen von zeitlich begrenzter Migration, dem dauerhaften Leben an mehreren Orten oder der wiederholten Migration. Immer mehr Menschen studieren oder arbeiten einige Zeit in einem anderen Land, oder sie arbeiten nach dem Studium in einem dritten; sie pendeln zwischen dem Leben mit ihrer Familie in einem und ihrer Arbeit in einem anderen Land, oder sie verlassen ihre Familie, um sie überhaupt versorgen zu können, und gehen dorthin, wo ihre Arbeitskraft gebraucht wird; oder aber Menschen, die ihr Leben an einem Ort verbracht haben, lassen sich erst im Ruhestand an einem anderen Ort nieder.

Migration wird für immer mehr Menschen ein Teil ihres Lebens und für alle Gesellschaften immer wichtiger. [...] Es geht vor allem darum, Mobilität und Migration nicht als Ausnahme, sondern als normale Tatsache zu begreifen. Blickt man in größeren historischen Zeiträumen zurück, ist die Bewegung von Menschen im Raum immer eine Normalität gewesen. [...] Menschen bewegen sich nicht nur, weil sie müssen, sondern auch, weil sie wollen. Manchmal brauchen sie dafür nicht einmal einen besonderen Grund, sondern folgen einfach einem Bedürfnis. Man muss nicht auf die stetig steigenden Zahlen von Urlaubsreisen verweisen. Für die allermeisten Menschen gilt, dass sie Reisen und die Möglichkeit zur räumlichen Veränderung genießen. [...]

Aus: Thomas Schwietering, Was ist Gesellschaft? Einführung in soziologische Grundbegriffe *(2011), UVK Verlagsgesellschaft/UTB, Konstanz, S. 30*

1 **Mediation** Your English penfriend wants to take part in a summer course in international politics. In her application for a place on the course, she has to write an essay about migration in Germany. She has found the definition above in a German textbook, but it is too difficult for her and she has asked for help from someone who speaks German. Write an email to sum up the main points of the text for her.

Beyond the text

2 Relate the information from the German textbook to the short stories you have read. Which form or forms of migration apply?

3 a Find out more about the term 'post-colonial literature'.

b Look back at the short stories you have read and discuss in what ways they can be seen as post-colonial literature.

4 a Describe the cartoon below.

Language help
gnome · fence · wheelbarrow · shovel · doner kebab

b Analyse the cartoon.

©Thomas Plaßmann

c Referring to the different forms of migration defined in the text on p. 86, discuss whether or not you feel that German culture has been transformed by migration. Refer to the cartoon and give three more examples.

C2 'Knowing Me' *Benjamin Zephaniah*

1 a Briefly explain the terms *identity* and *identity crisis*.
b Name possible reasons why someone would have an identity crisis.

Read the following poem and complete the tasks on p. 89.

According to de experts
I'm letting my side down,
Not playing the alienation game,
It seems I am too unfrustrated.
I have refused all counselling
I refuse to appear on daytime television
On night-time documentaries,
I'm not longing and yearning.
I don't have an identity crisis.

As I drive on poetic missions
On roads past midnight
I am regularly stopped by officers of the law
Who ask me to identify myself.
At times like these I always look into the mirror
Point
And politely assure them that
What I see is me.
I don't have an identity crisis.

I have never found the need
To workshop dis matter,
Or sit with fellow poets exorcising ghosts
Whilst searching for soulmates.
I don't wonder what will become of me
If I don't eat reggae food or dance to mango tunes,
Or think of myself as a victim of circumstance.
I'm the dark man, black man
With a brown dad, black man
Mommy is a red skin, black woman,
She don't have an identity crisis.

Being black somewhere else
Is just being black everywhere,
I don't have an identity crisis.
At least once a week I watch television
With my Jamaican hand on my Ethiopian heart
The African heart deep in my Brummie chest,
And I chant, Aston Villa, Aston Villa, Aston Villa,

1 de: (here) the
3 alienation [ˌeɪliəˈneɪʃn]: (here) feeling that you do not belong to a group
5 counselling: professional help, often therapy
8 yearn for sth./sb. [jɜːn]: want sth./sb. very much
12–18: referring to the 1980s policy of 'stop and search' ('sus law') in England and Wales which allowed the police to stop, search and arrest a person without evidence or warrant. It was aimed mainly at young Black men.
20 dis: this
35 Brummie (BE, infml): from the city of Birmingham in England
36 chant (v): sing or shout words and phrases
36 Aston Villa: English football club based in Aston, Birmingham

Believe me I know my stuff.
I am not wandering drunk into the rootless future
Nor am I going back in time to find somewhere to live.
I just don't want to live in a field with my past
Looking at blades of grass that look just like me, near a relic like me
Where the thunder is just like me, talking to someone just like me,
I don't just want to love me and only me; diversity is
  my pornography,
I want to make politically aware love with the rainbow.
Check dis Workshop Facilitator
Dis is me.
I don't have an identity crisis.

I have reached the stage where I can recognise my shadow.
I am quite pleased with myself.
When I'm sunbathing in Wales
I can see myself in India
As clearly as I see myself in Mexico.
I have now reached the stage
Where I am sick of people asking me if I feel British or West Indian,
African or Black, Dark and Lonely, Confused or Patriotic.
The thing is I don't feel lost,
I didn't even begin to look for myself until I met a social worker
And a writer looking for a subject
Nor do I write to impress poets.
Dis is not an emergency
I'm as kool as my imagination, I'm care more than your
  foreign policy.
I don't have an identity crisis.

I don't need an identity crisis to be creative,
I don't need an identity crisis to be oppressed.
I need love warriors and free minds wherever they are,
I need go getters and wide awakers for rising and shining,
I need to know that I can walk into any temple
Rave at any rave
Or get the kind of justice that my folk can see is just.

I am not half a poet shivering in the cold
Waiting for a culture shock to warm my long lost drum rhythm,
I am here and now, I am all that Britain is about
I'm happening as we speak.
Honestly,
I don't have an identity crisis.

From: Too Black, Too Strong *(2001), Bloodaxe Books Ltd., pp. 62–64*

41 blade of grass: (here) leaf of grass
41 relic [ˈrelɪk]: old object saved from the past
46 facilitator: person who helps sb. with their problems
60 impress sb.: *jdn. beeindrucken*
62 kool: cool
62 I'm care: I'm going to care
63 foreign policy: *Außenpolitik*
68 go-getter: person who is determined to succeed
72 shiver [ˈʃɪvə] (v): shake slightly

Info Benjamin Obadiah Iqbal Zephaniah

Benjamin Obadiah Iqbal Zephaniah (born 1958) is a British writer, poet, activist and musician. He grew up in Birmingham as the son of a Barbadian father and a Jamaican mother. He left school at age 13 because he was dyslexic. His dyslexia, however, did not stop him from performing poetry in church, which he had been doing since the age of 10. As a young man he got involved in a petty crime for which he received a criminal record and served a short prison sentence.
The music and the oral tradition of Jamaica strongly influence his poetry and he has recorded several albums of folk and reggae music. Calling himself a dub (Reggae) poet, he is famous for turning his poetry readings into concerts. His aim is to take poetry to people who do not normally read books, and he has successfully published works for children and young adults. The topics of his writing are various, reflecting his work as an activist against discrimination and animal abuse. As well as being voted the nation's third-favourite poet of all times in a BBC poll (and the only living one in the top ten), Zephaniah now holds 16 honorary degrees and has a hospital wing in East London named after him. Most recently he has played the role of Jeremiah Jesus in the BBC drama series *Peaky Blinders*.

Comprehension

2 Sum up each stanza of the poem in one or two sentences.

Analysis

3 Analyse the language of the poem, including spelling and the stylistic devices used.

4 Examine the speaker's perspective and speculate about the addressee of the poem (→ Info box, p. 29).

Beyond the text

5 Compare the speaker in the poem to the characters in the short stories you have read.

6 **Speaking** Work in pairs or in little groups. Imagine that one or more of the characters from the short stories is having a conversation with Benjamin Zephaniah about identity and multiculturalism. Act out the dialogue.

C3 The price of migrating *Gary Younge*

Read the text and complete the tasks on p. 92.

This is not a sob story. But the tears came anyhow. They crept up on me at the 70th birthday party of a friend a few years back. We were celebrating in a hotel ballroom in Letchworth in Hertfordshire and I had struck up a conversation with [a] distant acquaintance – a woman I had met only a few times before and have not met since. We talked about the primary school she worked at and the secondary school I went to […]. She asked me when I was going back to New York, where I'd been living for seven years at that point, and I told her, the next afternoon.

'You're so lucky,' she said. 'You've done so well for yourself. Your mum would be so proud.'

And that was when my eyes started welling up. Now it could have been any number of triggers – alcohol, jet lag or the mention of my mother, who died decades ago. But what really upset me was realising that in this town, people I wasn't even particularly close to knew me in a way that nobody else would. They knew place names that no one else in my regular life (apart from my brothers) knew. And yes, they not only knew my mother but they knew me when I had a mother.

The following day I would fly to a place where people knew a version of me where very little of any of this applied. My friends in New York knew I had brothers and had lost my mother. They knew I grew up working class in a town near London. The rest was footnotes – too much information for transient people, including myself who would soon move to Chicago, who were travelling light.

In short, I cried for bits of my life that had been lost. Not discarded; but atrophied. Huge, formative parts of my childhood and youth that I could no longer explain because you would really have had to have been there but without which I didn't make much sense.

Migration involves loss. Even when you're privileged, as I am, and move of your own free will, as I did, you feel it. Migrants, almost by definition, move with the future in mind. But their journeys inevitably involve excising part of their past. It's not workers who emigrate but people. And whenever they move they leave part of themselves behind. Efforts to reclaim that which has been lost result in something more than nostalgia but, if you're lucky, less than exile. And the losses keep coming. Funerals, christenings, graduations and weddings missed – milestones you couldn't make because your life is elsewhere.

If you're not lucky then your departure was forced by poverty, war or environmental disaster – or all three – and your destination is not of your choosing but merely where you could get to or where you were put. In that case the loss is bound to be all the more keen and painful. […] You may have to leave behind your partner, your kids and your

1 sob story [ˈsɒb]: sad story intended to make you cry
1 creep up on sb. (crept, crept) (v): *sich an jdn. anschleichen*
4 strike up a conversation (with sb.) (struck, struck): begin a conversation (with sb.)
4 acquaintance: *Bekannte(r)*
10 do well for yourself (infml): be successful
12 well up (v): fill with tears
13 trigger (n): *Auslöser*
20 apply: (here) be true
23 transient [ˈtrænziənt]: constantly moving
25 discard sth. (fml): throw sth. away
26 atrophy [ˈætrəfi] (v, fml): *verkümmern*
26 formative [ˈfɔːmətɪv]: *nachhaltig prägend*
30–31 by definition: (here) *wie es sich im Wort „Migrant" ausdrückt; wie schon die Bezeichnung „Migrant" besagt*
31 inevitably [ɪnˈevɪtəbli]: without exception
32 excise sth. [ɪkˈsaɪz] (fml): remove sth.
34 reclaim sth.: get sth. back
36 funeral: *Beerdigung*
36 christening [ˈkrɪsnɪŋ]: *Taufe*
36 graduation: *Schul-/ Hochschulabschlussfeier*
39 destination: place where sb. or sth. is going
41 keen: deep

home. In time, in order to survive, you may have to let go of your language, your religion and your sense of self. […]

I was lucky. I come from a travelling people. Those from an island as small as Barbados, buffeted by the winds of global economics and politics, tend to go where the work is. My great-grandfather helped build the Panama Canal. My parents came to England from Barbados in the early sixties. Of my 14 aunts and uncles nine left the island for significant periods of time. I have cousins in Canada, Britain, the US and the Caribbean, some of whom I've never met. […]

I fell in love with an American and here we are. My sense of loss is primarily cultural. Tapping a football to my son in the park and watching him pick it up ('Kick it! Kick it!' I'd implore); asking why there's an armed policeman in his elementary school ('It's a good question,' said my wife. 'But that's not particularly remarkable here'); seeing nieces and nephews grow up on Facebook; returning for a holiday to find all the teenagers you know wearing onesies and using catchphrases from shows you've never heard of; seeing or hearing something that reminds you of home, your first home, and realising you lack too many common reference points to share it with those with whom you share your life now.

Migration is a good thing, so long as it is voluntary. I believe in the free movement of people. But that's not to say it doesn't have a price. I have choices that most of the world's migrants don't have. I can go back. And I'm happy where I am.

This is not a sob story. But every now and then, when I least expect them, the tears come anyhow.

From: As migrants we leave home in search for a future, but we lose the past, *The Guardian, 24 March 2015*

46 buffet sb./sth. [ˈbʌfɪt]: hit sb./sth.
53 tap sth.: (here) kick sth. lightly
54 implore: *flehentlich bitten*
56 remarkable: unusual
58 onesie [ˈwʌnzi]: jumpsuit
58 catchphrase: popular slogan
59 show: (here) TV show
61 reference point: *Bezugspunkt*

Info Gary Younge

Gary Andrew Younge (born 1969), from Hertfordshire in southern England, is of Barbadian ancestry. He is a journalist, columnist, author, broadcaster and academic. After his journalism studies, for which he received a scholarship from *The Guardian* newspaper, he did a short internship at Yorkshire Televison. In 1993, he started working for *The Guardian*, eventually becoming an important editor. Younge became Professor of sociology at the University of Manchester in April 2020. Even though he had to leave his position at *The Guardian* to accept the professorship, he plans on continuing to write part-time for the newspaper.

Comprehension

1 Use the space below to create a mind map in which you collect the different meanings of identity as explained by Younge in his essay.

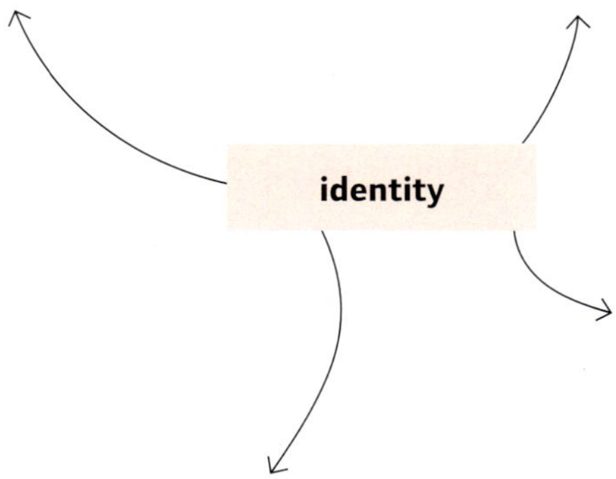

Analysis

2 **a** Explain what Younge means when he writes that migration always comes at a price (cf. ll. 63–64).

b Writing Comment on Younge's view, referring to one or more of the stories from this collection.

Module II

Gran Torino

Part A
Pre-viewing activities

A1 Working with a film poster

1 Work in pairs and look for film posters from *Gran Torino* online.

a Each choose a different film poster and imagine what kind of film *Gran Torino* might be. Examine the aspects below and say how they influence your predictions. Make notes.

the colors and shading used — the title of the film — the person/people on the poster

the font (style and size of the letters) — the images used on the poster

b Compare your predictions with your partner. Discuss what aspects of the posters influenced them.

A2 Imagining a scenario

1 **Writing** Write a short interior monologue for the character on your poster (→ Info box, p. 134).

Part B
While-viewing activities

B1 Getting into the film

Making predictions

1 Describe the situation that is shown in the photo below. How do people act and what might they think during a situation like this one?

Comprehension

2 **Viewing** Watch the exposition (→ Info box) of *Gran Torino* (0:00:00–00:17:20). Pay special attention to the following questions:
- What characters are introduced?
- What clashes might arise?

Info The exposition of a film
In films, as in drama, the opening sequence contains important information.
The viewers are introduced to the setting, to the main characters and their relationships, to previous events that determine the plot of the film, and often also to the central conflict that the film will be dealing with. This opening sequence is called the exposition (→ Info box, p. 134).

3 Work in pairs. One of you works on task **a** and the other on task **b**.

a As you watch the segment, make notes on the following questions about Walt. Fill in the information in the table below.

What is Walt's full name? What does his last name tell us about his family's origin?	
What do you find out about his family? How is his relationship with them?	
What is his religion and his attitude towards it?	
What do you know about his past?	
How does he live? What is his neighborhood like? What does he think about his neighborhood?	
How would you describe Walt's character?	
What does he value in life?	
What makes Walt struggle to belong?	

b As you watch the segment, make notes on the following questions about Thao. Fill the information in the table below.

What is Thao's family like? What is Thao's role in his family?	
What does Thao's family think of him?	
How would you describe Thao's character?	
What is his relationship with his cousin and his gang? What is his attitude towards them?	
How does he experience his neighborhood, especially Walt?	
What makes Thao struggle to belong?	

c Exchange your results with your partner.

Analysis

4 a A well-made film often works with contrasts and similarities. Watch the following scenes again closely and describe how this technique is used here:
- 00:07:46–00:08:05
- 00:10:33–00:11:21

b Discuss with a partner what these scenes show about the question of belonging.

c Write a short text in which you describe the contrasts and similarities in the two scenes and analyse their impact on the question of belonging. → Language help

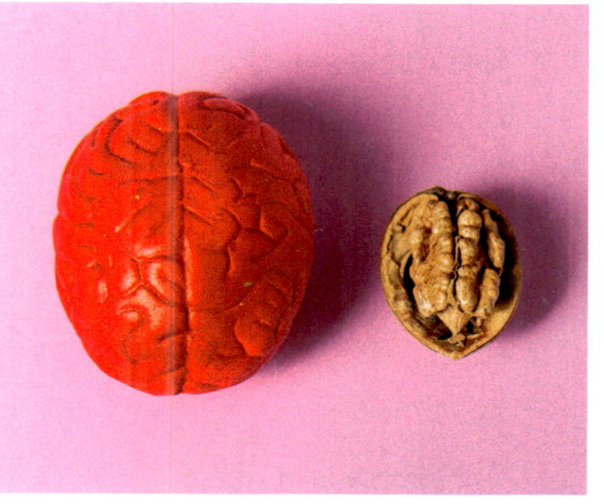

Language help

while … • whereas … • in contrast to … • contrary to … • unlike … • both … • like … • have in common … • similar … • in the same way … • also … • thus …

Beyond the text

5 Work on **a** or **b**.

a Writing Write a role biography from Walt's point of view (→ Info box 'Role biography'). Use the information you collected in task **3a** (p. 95). Add his thoughts and opinions where appropriate. The following questions should be addressed:
- What has shaped Walt's identity so far?
- In what areas is his identity put into question?

Info Role biography

When writing a role biography, you are writing about one particular character's life.
- Put yourself in the character's shoes and use the first person perspective.
- Write like a diary. Talk about your family and your relationship to them, your everyday life, your neighborhood, your past, and your hopes for the future; tell your reader what is important to you and what causes you problems.
- Write a text in complete sentences.

b Writing After Spider and his gang have shown Thao the Gran Torino, he is left alone. What goes on in his mind? Write an interior monologue (→ Info box, p. 173). Use information you collected in task **3b** (p. 96).
The following questions should be addressed:
- What factors are shaping Thao's identity?
- When and how is his identity challenged?

6 The film is set in 21st century USA. In order to better understand it, it is important to have some background knowledge.

a Split into groups of four. Select one of the topics below.

A Detroit and its automotive industry

B The Gran Torino and American muscle cars

C The Korean War

D The Hmong and their culture

E The Hmong in the USA

F Polish immigration to the USA

G Youth gangs in Detroit

b Find out about your group's topic and create a poster on which you present important information. Add images, timelines, etc.

c **Speaking** Present your poster to the class.

d Hang your posters on the classroom wall. They should stay there for reference while you continue dealing with the film.

B2 Shifting alliances

Making predictions

1 **Speaking** Work in pairs.

a After you've worked on the exposition, talk about how the story might continue. Make predictions on what role the Gran Torino is going to play.

b Join another pair. Present your ideas and discuss which of the suggested predictions is most likely.

c Present your findings in class.

Comprehension

2 **Viewing** Watch the segment from 00:12:08 to 00:36:51.

a Summarize what is happening in the scenes by completing the sentences below.

Two gangs (00:12:09–00:14:52)

A Thao is walking along the street and reading a book when teenagers in a car

____.

B Thao's cousin Fong and his gang ____.

C After the first gang leaves, Fong ____.

1972 Gran Torino (00:14:52–00:17:20)

D Thao and Fong meet again at Thao's house. Fong tries to convince Thao to join their gang; to become a member, Thao would have to ______________________________

____.

Life and death (00:17:21–00:19:49)

E Father Janovich and Walt meet in a bar. When the topic of life and death comes up, Walt tells him about ______________________________

____.

Light in the garage (00:19:50–00:20:58)

F Walt wakes up in the middle of the night and ______________________________.

G Thao ____.

'Get off my lawn!' (00:22:53–00:25:04)

H Thao and Sue are sitting on their porch when Fong and his friends pass by. When they try to force Thao to do his test of courage, his family gets out of the house and they all get into a fight. Walt ______________________________.

I Fong and his gang ______________________________.

J The neighbors ______________________________.

Hero in the neighborhood (00:25:05–00:29:17)

K The next day people ______________________________.

L Walt ____.

M Thao ____.

Hmong people (00:30:01–00:36:51)

N Sue and her date Trey ______________________________.

O Walt ____.

b Compare the storyline with the one you predicted.

3 Viewing Go back to the scene in which Spider and his gang try to persuade Thao to join them for the first time (00:15:00–00:17:19).

a List the reasons for joining a gang mentioned in this scene.

b Describe Spider's character (→ Info box, p. 151).

4 Listening Watch the final scene of the segment again (00:34:47–00:36:51). Complete the following sentences by ticking the correct item.

a Walt thinks Sue shouldn't be walking around in that neighborhood because …

A it's a smart and posh neighborhood.
B she might fall into the river.
C she might get killed.
D it's not an Asian neighborhood.

b Walt thinks Sue shouldn't date Trey because …

A he finds him stupid.
B Trey does not belong to her community.
C she's not good enough for him.
D her community will not approve of him.

c Hmong is …

A a place.
B a people.
C a part of Laos.
D between Laos, Thailand and China.

d The Hmong came to the USA because of …

A the prosecution of communists in their country.
B their involvement with the Vietnam war.
C the long winters in the Midwest.
D the living conditions in the jungle.

e Hmong girls in the US …

A rarely know which direction to go in life.
B quickly adopt US culture.
C usually are good students.
D often get into conflict with the law.

Analysis

5 Examine Walt's and Sue's attitude to the Hmong and to each other in the dialogue from task **4** (p. 100). Look closely at the way they both talk about themselves and each other.

6 In this segment you are introduced to several young people who belong to different ethnic groups.

a Make a list of the qualities and symbols the individual groups have to signify that someone belongs to those groups.

	Group: ______	Group: ______	Group: ______
Qualities			
Symbols			

b List situations in the film in which an individual clearly does not belong to a group and explain how this is noticeable.

Beyond the text

7 **Writing** Imagine that you are Trey at the end of the day in which he and Sue get harassed by a group of black teenagers (00:30:00–00:34:46). Write Sue an email explaining what went through your head during that moment and commenting on why you felt helpless.

B3 Gang culture

1 **Mediation** You have been emailing your tandem partner in California about why young people join gangs. Your tandem partner came across the article below and needs help understanding it. Read the article and write an email to your tandem partner in which you summarize in English why Hakan wanted to be in a gang.

Leben in einer Kreuzberger Türkengang *Matern Boeselager*

Kind von Immigranten, Gangmitglied, jüngster Bankräuber Deutschlands: Wir haben uns mit dem ehemaligen „36 Boy" Killa Hakan über seine Vergangenheit unterhalten.

In Berlin sind die 36 Boys Legende. Die Gang bestand hauptsächlich aus den Kindern türkischer Gastarbeiter und hatte ihr Revier um das Kottbusser Tor und die Naunynstraße. In den 80ern sorgte ihr Name regelmäßig für Schnappatmung bei Berliner Innenpolitikern, Polizeichefs und *Spiegel*-Reportern. […]

Hakan Durmuş, auch „Killa Hakan" genannt, war von Anfang an dabei. Wenn man wissen will, wie es sich wirklich anfühlt, als Mitglied einer Kreuzberger Türkengang aufzuwachsen, gibt es also kaum einen besseren Gesprächspartner – schließlich lebt Hakan immer noch in der Naunynstraße. […] Ich habe mich mit ihm über seine Kindheit im Berliner Gastarbeitermilieu, Massenschlägereien zwischen Türkengangs und über Möchtegern-36er wie Deso Dogg und Tim Raue unterhalten.

VICE: Hakan, warum heißt du eigentlich Killa?

Killa Hakan: Na, weil ich immer korrekt war. Wenn was schön war, hat man früher gesagt: „Mann, Killa Auto, Killa Mädchen." Killa Hakan!

Bist du in Kreuzberg geboren?

Ich bin Ur-Kreuzberger. Geboren im Urbankrankenhaus, von da bin ich sofort in die Naunynstraße gekommen. Besser geht's nicht mehr.

Wie sah die Gegend hier damals aus?

Das war dunkel hier. Das war ja hier direkt an der Mauer. Keiner wollte hier was mieten. Nur die Kanaken sollten dahin, die machen das schon. Und wir haben das gemacht!

Wie war das, damals hier als Kind von Gastarbeitern aufzuwachsen?

Wir sind jedes Jahr in die Türkei gefahren. Also, wir waren hier in der Schule und so, aber wir wussten von den Eltern, wenn wir genug Geld für ein Haus haben, dann gehen wir zurück in die Türkei. Mit dem Gedanken sind wir aufgewachsen, jeder von uns.

Die wollten auch wirklich gehen, aber dann kam '82 der Putsch. Da haben die in der Türkei gefragt: „Bist du links oder rechts?" Wenn du falsch geantwortet hast, warst du weg. Also haben die Eltern gesagt: Wir lassen unsere Kinder in Europa. Wer will schon seine Kinder verlieren? Also mussten wir plötzlich alle umdenken, da mussten wir uns schon hart umstellen. […]

Wie hat das mit der Gang angefangen?
Da muss ich 12, 13 gewesen sein. Wie gesagt, als der Putsch kam, da wussten wir erstmal alle nicht, was tun. Wir waren sauer. Wir hatten nicht mal deutsche Freunde – was sollen wir mit denen, wir gehen ja sowieso wieder, dachten wir vorher.

Aber in die Diskos wollten wir natürlich. Nur: Wir sind ja Moslems, wir hatten das nicht gelernt. Und wir sind natürlich nicht reingelassen worden – wer will schon sechs, sieben Kanaken reinlassen? Immer gab es Stress, immer gab es Scheiße. Da haben wir gesagt: „OK, ihr lasst uns nicht rein? Wir kommen aber rein." So kam dann die Gang.
Was habt ihr dann gemacht?
Erstmal: Kotti sichern. Erstmal klarmachen, das hier ist unseres. Wir wollten, dass uns da, wo wir wohnen, jeder akzeptiert. Durch die Gang warst du halt nicht mehr alleine, da waren dann noch vier andere, die waren genau so wie du. Dann kommt es auch nicht mehr so hart, wenn jemand „dreckige Kanaken" sagt. Dann macht dich das stark, das hört sich dann ganz anders an. So hat das ganz früher angefangen, die 36 Boys.

From: 'Mit dem Baseballschläger gegen Nazis: Aufwachsen in einer Berliner Türkengang', Vice Online, *5 May 2015*

Analysis

2 Work in pairs. One of you works on task **a** and the other works on task **b**. When you are finished, do task **c** together.
- **a** Compare Spider with Hakan. Consider the aspects in Spider's life that are not shown, such as his life as a child (→ Language help, p. 97).
- **b** Compare Hakan with Sue, especially their situations and attitudes. (→ Language help, p. 97)
- **c** Compare your results. Discuss whether Hakan's situation is more similar to Spider's or to Sue's.

Beyond the text

3 Split the class into four groups. Each group works on a different character: Thao, Sue, Spider or Walt.
- **a** In your groups, prepare to play the role of your character. Prepare to introduce yourself to the others, to share your opinion on gangs and to answer questions about your opinion. Gather all the information available on that character.
- **b** Prepare questions to ask the other three characters (→ Language help).

Language help

What did you feel when …? • Why did you …? • What do you think of …? • Do you regret …? • Are you proud of …? • Explain … • Would you …? • How do you feel about …?

c **Speaking** Form new groups of four. Each group needs to contain one student from each of the original groups. As your character, introduce yourself to the group. Then the other group members ask you the questions they prepared.

d Remain in character and discuss the following question with the new group: 'Gangs – a surrogate for families?'

Annotation
surrogate: sth. used instead of sth. else

B4 A shifting sense of identity

Making predictions

1 Take seven large sheets of paper. Write one of the following topics in the middle of each sheet and place them on different tables in the classroom.

food

peer relationships

family

birthday/family celebrations

cultural conventions / respecting others

names

religion

a Now walk around in the room and stop at different tables. Write down what the topic means to you. Consider how it shapes your identity.

b Notice what the others have written and add your own thoughts if you wish. Do not talk.

2 Split into seven groups. Each group is assigned one of the topics from task **1**.

a Read the comments on your poster and discuss them in your group.

b Summarize your findings in no more than three sentences and present them to the class, speaking in the name of the group, i.e. 'To many of us, family means …', 'Food is to us …', etc.

c How do you think these topics will be further developed in the film? Discuss with the class.

Comprehension

3 **Viewing** Continue watching the film (00:36:52–00:52:34).
  a Keep working in your groups and make notes on what happens in relation to the topic you worked on in task **2** (p. 104).
  b Discuss your results in your group.
  c **Speaking** Present your results to the class.

Analysis

4 **a** In your groups, discuss how the information you found affects the characters' identity.
  b **Speaking** Present your results to the class.

Beyond the text

5 When Walt goes to the lavatory to wash his face at his neighbor's party, he makes an important realization.
  a What does he realize about himself, his family and the Hmong?
  b Analyse how props and camera perspective underline the importance of this realization.
  c **Writing** Write a blog post in which you explain Walt's realization in the context of the scene, comment on it and examine what factors may have contributed to it.

6 **Writing** Imagine Walt goes for another haircut. He tells Martin, the barber, about his visit to the neighbors' house on his birthday. He becomes thoughtful and starts reflecting on his sense of belonging. Write this scene. It should primarily be a monologue by Walt, but Martin may throw in a few words here or there.

B5 Male worlds in *Gran Torino*

Making predictions

Before watching the next segment of the film, read the following info box about stereotypes.

Info Stereotypes

A stereotype is a fixed and often overly generalized belief one has about a particular group of people regarding their gender, ethnicity, class, sexual identity, etc. The negative consequences of stereotypes are clear – they lead to prejudice against and discrimination of certain groups. At the same time, they can help you reduce the complexity of the world. For example, most societies have clear ideas of how women and men should behave. Identifying the person you are talking to as male or female will help you understand and anticipate their behavior in very many cases. Likewise, stereotypes can create a sense of belonging to a group – fitting into a group that is defined e.g. by masculinity or femininity can create a sense of identity.

1 Think of the way women and men are portrayed in *Gran Torino*. Work in pairs and fill in the table below with examples of gender roles and expectations from the movie.

Gender roles and expectations in *Gran Torino*: men	**Gender roles and expectations in *Gran Torino*: women**

a **Speaking** Present your examples to the class.

b Discuss the following with your classmates:
- Find examples of gender stereotypes in your own society.
- Name examples of behaviors that contradict these stereotypes.
- How might the topic of gender stereotypes be addressed in the rest of the movie?

Comprehension

2 **Viewing** Watch the next segment of the film (00:52:35–01:29:58) and answer the following questions:

a Why is it important for Thao's family that he does some work for Walt?

b What kind of jobs does Thao do for Walt?

c Why does Walt call his son Mitch?

d Why does Walt sell Thao his old freezer at a cheaper price?

e What helps Mr Kennedy decide to give Thao a job?

3 **Viewing** Before watching again, take a look at sentences **a–f** below. Then go back to the scene in which Walt and Thao are in the garden, speaking about work (01:07:53–01:10:23). While you watch, complete the following sentences by ticking the correct item. There s only one possible answer per sentence beginning.

a The Hmong consider this to be women's work:

A watching birds.
B preparing food.
C cleaning the house.
D taking care of the garden.

b Thao thinks that Walt should quit …

A smoking.
B gardening.
C being in a gang.
D making fun of him.

c Walt's lighter has a symbol that represents …

A the fifties.
B his very first car.
C his time in the army.
D one of his favorite bands.

d Walt used to install these on Gran Torinos:

A the gearing wheel.
B the steering wheel.
C the gearing column.
D the steering column.

e Thao is not optimistic about going to university because it …

A is expensive.
B would cost him his time.
C is not needed to work in sales.
D would force him to leave his family.

f Walt thinks that Thao could get a job in construction because …

A You would like it.
B it doesn't require specific qualifications.
C he knows people who work in that field.
D he's quite skilled with his hands.

Analysis

4 a Examine how the men in this segment behave.
Pay special attention to:
- Walt
- Thao
- Martin
- Tim Kennedy
- the members of the Hmong gang

Focus on the following aspects:
- the way they talk
- their ideas of suitable work
- the way they treat others
- the role violence plays in their lives

b Compare and discuss your answers in class.

c Compare the men's behavior in the film to the way men act in your society. Do they act a certain way to belong?

B6 Realigning the stars

Making predictions

1 Watch the last few minutes of the previous segment again (01:24:58–01:29:58). How might the story go on from here?

Comprehension

2 Viewing Read the following incomplete sentences, then watch the final segment of the film (01:29:59–end) and fill in the gaps based on what you see.

A Walt ______________________ his lawn.

B He takes ______________________.

C He goes to ______________ in order to ______________.

D He buys ______________________.

E He goes to ______________________.

F He cleans ______________________________.

G He gives Thao a ______________________________.

H He talks with Thao about ______________________________.

I He locks ____________________ in the ____________________.

J He leaves ______________________________ with Thao's grandmother.

K He calls up ______________________________.

L He goes to ______________________________'s house.

M He takes a ______________________________ from his pocket.

N He points his ____________________ at ____________________.

O He reaches into his jacket to pull out a ______________________________.

Analysis

3 **a** Explain Walt's plan and his reasons for acting the way he does. Do so in 3–5 sentences.
b Compare your text with another student.
c Find another pair of students to work with and compare your results once again.
d Discuss any open questions in class.

4 Watch the scene from 01:39:30–01:44:15 again and analyse the way it is presented. Consider e. g. camera work, light, music and sound. Examine to what effect these means are employed and say how suitable you find them.

5 Examine Walt's attitude towards religion in this segment, taking into account observations you made while watching the whole film.

6 Walt's actions and will, which is read at the end of the film, can be seen as a statement on his sense of belonging.
Get together in groups of four. Work with a placemat.
a Write down your thoughts on this question: Where does Walt feel he belongs? Compare situations when Walt's sense of belonging stayed the same to when it shifted.
b Rotate the placemat three times so that each student can read the others' thoughts and comment on them in writing.
c Together with your group, formulate a statement on Walt's sense of belonging in three sentences. These should contain the essence of all four contributions.
d **Speaking** Present your statements in class and discuss them.

Beyond the text

6 Imagine that Sue and Thao are sitting together after Walt's funeral, talking about Walt and the past events. They reflect on how their lives and their identities have been affected. Work with a partner to prepare this role-play. One of you works on task **a**, the other works on task **b**. Complete tasks **c** and **d** together.

a Prepare the role of Sue (→ Language help).
Consider the following questions:
- How did she experience Walt?
- What are her memories of the encounter with the African-American gang?
- How did she experience the Hmong gang?
- Where does she feel she belongs?
- How did her identity change throughout the past events?

Language help
In my experience … · My experience was … · It was a scary/difficult/happy time in my life because … · Looking back, I … · I feel like I belong / don't belong because …

b Prepare the role of Thao (→ Language help, p. 97).
Consider the following questions:
- How did he experience Walt?
- How did he experience the Hmong gang?
- Where does he feel he belongs?
- How did his identity change throughout the past events?
- How has inheriting the Gran Torino affected him and his identity?

c **Speaking** Get together and practice the dialogue between Sue and Thao.

d **Speaking** Present it to the class.

B7 Working with a film title

1 **a** Comment on the relevance of the film's title. Consider the following aspects and give reasons for your opinion:
- Where in the film does the car play an important role?
- What is the importance of the car for Walt's and Thao's identity?

b Collect your ideas and discuss them with a partner.

Part C
Post-viewing activities

C1 Writing a film review

1 Write your own review of the film *Gran Torino* with the title: '*Gran Torino* – Shifting identities' (→ Info box).
  a Collect ideas. Consider different characters (Walt, Thao, Sue, Spider, etc.) and some areas that shape their identities (e.g. family, neighborhood, religion, gangs, names, gender, work, material values, symbols of belonging, etc.). Do not try to cover all characters or areas. Instead, select those that are most important to you.
  b Sort your ideas into paragraphs that contain the relevant elements of a review.
  c **Writing** Write your review.
  d In a group of four, exchange your reviews and give each other feedback (your teacher will provide you with suitable feedback forms).

Info Writing a film review
In a film review, you provide information on a film you have watched and express your opinion about it – you either recommend it or discourage people from seeing it.
In order to prepare the review, make notes on interesting, very good or very bad aspects while watching the film. Collect important information such as the director's name, important actors, its running time. For the specific task above, choose exemplary scenes in which characters struggle to form their identity.
Structure your ideas. Then, in the introduction, give some basic information on the film and on questions of identity as a central theme in it. In the main part of the review, briefly summarize the film's plot and comment on relevant aspects, especially on how the characters deal with their shifting identities.
Finally, give a summary of your opinion in the conclusion, possibly also recommending your film for a specific target group.

Module III

Richard III

Part A
Pre-reading activities

A1 The Bard of Avon

Info William Shakespeare (1564–1616)
Shakespeare is widely regarded as the greatest writer in the English language. He was born and brought up in Stratford-upon-Avon, England, where he married and had three children. He then moved to London, and, by 1592, he had become known as a playwright and was beginning his acting career in the theatres of London. In 1594 he formed the Lord Chamberlain's Men with a group of actors, which soon became the leading company in London. In 1599, they built their own theatre, the Globe, on the south bank of the River Thames. After the death of Queen Elizabeth in 1603, the company was awarded a royal patent by King James I and changed its name to The King's Men.
Shakespeare produced most of his known work between 1589 and 1613. His early plays were mainly comedies and histories, like *Richard III* (~1595). Until about 1608 he wrote primarily tragedies, which were then followed by romances. In 1623, two of his former colleagues published the *First Folio*, a collected edition of his dramatic works that included all but two of his plays. His sonnets were published in 1609.
Shakespeare appears to have retired to Stratford around 1613 at age 49. He died three years later. Few records of his private life survive, and there has been much speculation about his physical appearance, sexuality, religious beliefs, and whether the works attributed to him were written by others. His surviving work consists of about 38 plays, 154 sonnets and several other poems. His plays are performed worldwide more often than those of any other playwright.

1 a Research the following topics:

- Elizabeth I and her time
- Renaissance London
- Shakespeare's family and education
- Shakespeare's Stratford
- Elizabethan theatre
- The original Globe Theatre
- Shakespeare's theatre troupes
- Shakespeare's history plays
- Shakespeare's other plays

b **Speaking** Present your findings to the class.

2 a Research the concepts of the *Chain of Being*, the *Wheel of Fortune*, the *Four Humours* and the *Zodiac Man*.

b **Speaking** Your school's English department wants to include information about the Elizabethan world view on the school's website. Create a podcast or a short video for the website in which you explain the Elizabethan world view while referring to the concepts from **a**.

Bottles with the four humours that, according to Hippocratic medicine, needed to be in balanced proportions for a body to be healthy

A2 Imagining Richard

1 a Find production photos showing actors Antony Sher, Laurence Olivier, Kevin Spacey and Ian McKellen as Richard III.

b Discuss what is suggested about:
- their costumes
- the setting of the play
- Richard's disability
- their interpretation of the character.

c Shakespeare describes Richard as a severely disabled man with a hunchback, a shrunken arm and a limp. Discuss whether you think that the production photos from **a** fit this description.

A3 The historical Richard

1 a Read the info box on the Tudor Myth.

Info The Tudor Myth

The Tudor Myth refers to a tradition in English literature to present the onset of Tudor reign (established through King Henry VII in 1485) as a golden era of prosperity and peace that put an end to the turmoil and relentless fight for the crown dominating England in the 15th century – especially under Richard III.

The Tudor Myth goes back to King Henry VII, who had only a shaky claim to the English throne. To strengthen his position, he encouraged historians to blacken Richard III's name and to praise the Tudors for bringing peace to the country. This Tudor Myth has shaped the traditional idea of Richard as an evil, despotic tyrant and killer of children.

b Do some research on the real Richard's life and reign on the website of the *Richard III Society*, an organization that seeks to clear his name posthumously.

c Design a presentation on Richard based on what you learned in **b**.

d **Speaking** Present your findings to the class.

2 **Listening** In 2012, Richard III's skeleton was found under a car park in Leicester. Find and watch the TEDx Talk 'Richard III: solving a 500-year-old cold case' about the discovery.

a Listen closely to 0:00–2:30 and fill in the missing information in the table below.

Annotations:
- choir: part of a church where the singers sit
- Greyfriars: *Franziskanerkloster in Leicester*
- dissolution of monasteries: closure of all religious houses in England between 1536 and 1541 ordered by Henry VIII
- badger sb. (infml): ask sb. to do sth. insistently

A What was done to Richard's body after his death:	1 ______________________ 2 ______________________ 3 ______________________
B What a rumour said about Richard's grave after the dissolution of monasteries:	4 ______________________ 5 ______________________
C What the dissolution of monasteries meant for Richard's grave:	6 ______________________

b Sum up what is said about the archaeological dig as well as the DNA confirmation of Richard's identity.

A4 Trippingly on the tongue

1 Shakespeare wrote his plays mostly in blank verse, i.e. verses with a regular rhythm of ten beats and no rhyme.

a **Viewing** Go online, find and watch the TED Ex video 'Why Shakespeare loved iambic pentameter'.

b **Speaking** Work in teams. Take turns reading the following lines from *Richard III* out loud, applying what you learned in the video from **a**. Correct each other if needed.

'A happy and a joyful time of day!' (Act IV, Scene 1, l. 6)

'O wonderful, when devils tell the truth!' (Act I, Scene 2, l. 73)

'That bottled spider, that foul bunch-backed toad.' (Act IV, Scene 4, l. 81)

'True hope is swift and flies with swallow's wings.' (Act V, Scene 2, l. 23)

Part B
While-reading and viewing activities

Shakespeare wrote eight plays about the historical struggle for the English throne between the House of York and the House of Lancaster, two hostile branches of the royal Plantagenet dynasty, which ended with the Wars of the Roses (1455–1485). *Richard III* is the final play of this series.
The play shows the Yorkist Richard, at present the Duke of Gloucester, in his unstoppable pursuit of power. After their victory over the Lancastrians in the Battle of Tewkesbury, the other Yorkists are celebrating their victory.

Scene from a re-enactment of the Battle of Tewkesbury, one of the decisive battles of the Wars of the Roses (1471)

B1 The spin doctor 1 (Act I, Scene 1, ll. 1–41)

Richard enters to express his feelings about the victory.

Read his famous opening monologue (Act I, Scene 1, ll. 1–41).

Comprehension

1 Complete the sentences below.

A Apart from Richard, all the people react to the victory by ______________________________

____.

B Richard cannot take part because ______________________________

____.

C As a consequence, he has determined ______________________________

____.

D To start his newly devised campaign, he ______________________________

____.

Analysis

2 Richard uses a lot of rhetorical devices in his monologue to make his words more memorable and to involve the audience, which he turns into his co-conspirators. Identify examples of antithesis, repetition, exaggeration, personification, dramatic or emotive words, and metaphors that contribute to these effects.

Beyond the text

3 a In groups of three or four, perform the speech in various styles (e. g. angry, self-congratulatory, ironic, whispering). Add gestures and movements Richard could make.

b Decide which style is most suitable in which part of the monologue.

c Compare your version to the one from Richard Loncraine's film *Richard III* from 1995 (cf. 00:09:22–00:12:06). Discuss which aspects of both you find most effective.

4 **Speaking** Imagine you were to cast an actor for a film version of the play. Choose a well-known actor and give a short presentation to the director trying to convince him/her that the person you have chosen is best for the role of Richard.

B2 The spin doctor 2 (Act I, Scene 1, ll. 42–161)

Read the rest of the scene.

Comprehension

1 Complete the sentences below.

A Richard suggests that Clarence's accuser is ______________________________

because ______________________________.

B Richard promises Clarence ______________________________

______________________________.

C Alone, however, Richard confides that ______________________________

______________________________.

D Hastings enters and tells Richard that ______________________________

______________________________.

E Richard reveals more wicked plots. He intends to ______________________________

and to ______________________________.

Analysis

2 Examine the picture Richard paints of his brothers and the women at court.

3 Give examples of Richard's irony in this scene.

B3 The seducer (Act I, Scene 2)

Read Scene 2.

Comprehension

1 Decide whether the following statements are true or false.

	True	False
A Lady Anne follows her husband's coffin.		
B Anne curses the killer and his family.		
C Anne calls her dead husband 'gentle, mild and virtuous'.		
D Anne doesn't know who stabbed her husband.		
E She slaps Richard's face.		
F Richard offers to stab himself if Anne doesn't want to kill him.		
G Richard has the coffin carried to its destined place.		
H Due to his success, Richard thinks less critically of himself.		

2 Finish the sentences and give evidence for the following statements.

A Lady Anne truly loves her dead husband: she says about him that lines:

____. ____________

B Richard speaks about sexual love when he expresses his wish to lines:

____. ____________

C Using the typical language of a wooing suitor, Richard says lines:

(1) ________________________, (2) ________________ ____________

________________ and (3) ____________________.

D Richard even tells Anne that for the first time in his life he lines:

(1) ____ and ____________

(2) ____.

E He claims he killed her husband and King Henry VI because lines:

____. ____________

F Lady Anne accepts Richard's ring because he remarks how it lines:

____. ____________

Analysis

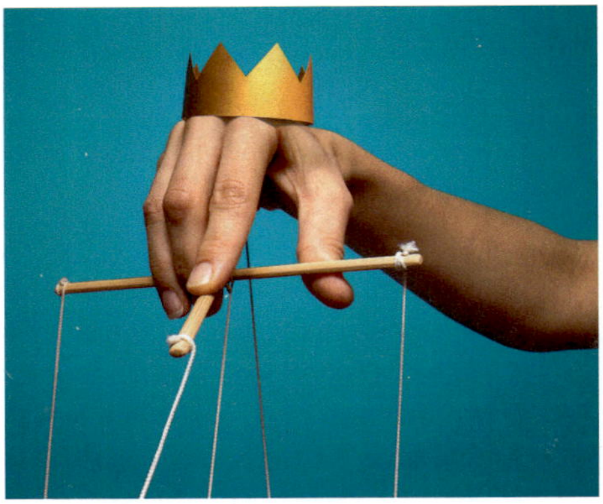

3 Typical strategies people use to manipulate the truth are:
- the denial of proven facts
- misrepresentations or lies
- insincere flattery
- blaming others for one's own actions
- grandiose gestures.

Give examples of Richard's deceptive strategies in his dialogue with Anne.

4 Anne insults Richard by referring to his physical appearance, his evil deeds and his Satan-like character. Collect five insults for each aspect.

Beyond the text

5 Lady Anne's complete change of opinion has perplexed many viewers.

a In groups of three or four, speculate about why she accepts Richard's ring.

Language help
feel guilty • be attracted to sb. • be scheming • have a 'bad boy' charm • feel flattered • feel defenceless • fall for a trickster's deceit • play for time • be emotionally exhausted with grief • resist sb. • be calculating

b **Speaking** Prepare different readings of her text and decide which is the most convincing.

6 **Writing** Imagine you are an agony aunt and Anne has written a letter asking for advice on whether she should marry Richard. Write a letter giving her your advice.

Making predictions

7 What do you think Anne's answer will be to Richard's marriage proposal?

B4 The opponent (Act I, Scene 3, from l. 43)

At the royal palace, Queen Elizabeth, wife of the newly crowned King Edward IV, worries about her sickly husband. In the case of his death, the closest male relative would rule the country as Lord Protector until her son Edward became old enough to take over the throne. With Clarence in prison that would be Richard. The queen fears this outcome because Richard is openly critical of Elizabeth's family, the Woodvilles.

Read Scene 3, beginning with Richard's entrance.

Comprehension

1 The action of the scene is summed up in the statements A–G. Put them in the correct order by writing numbers on the right.

Statement	Order
A Richard gloats over his success in incriminating the Woodvilles and sowing discord between them and the other noble lords.	____
B Elizabeth is outraged and threatens to inform King Edward. Richard counters this by reminding her of the support he gave the Yorkist side during the war, whereas the Woodvilles fought on the Lancastrian, i. e. their enemy's, side.	____
C Old Queen Margaret voices her anger at the company present, but is told that she deserves her fate since she too has committed cruel deeds in wartime.	____
D Richard warns the two murderers not to be moved by Clarence's pleas for mercy and they promise to carry out their business promptly.	____
E Richard finds some charitable words to pity Margaret's unhappy fate and lament Clarence's arrest.	____
F Richard blames Queen Elizabeth for his brother Clarence's and Lord Hastings's imprisonment. He also criticizes her for granting great privileges and titles to her Woodville family, who are not of genuine noble birth.	____
G Margaret curses everyone, apart from Buckingham, and prophesies sorrow, downfall and death for her listeners.	____

Analysis

2 Look at the first three scenes of this act. Examine how Shakespeare characterizes Richard (→ Info box, p. 151).

Language help

lure sb. into complicity • gleeful • ruthless • scheming • misogynistic • narcissistic • unattractive exterior • gloat over sth. • hypocritical • ambitious • malevolent • cunning • sarcastic • deceive sb. • disdainful • malicious joy • unrepentant • eloquent • treacherous

3 Analyse the role the three royal women Elizabeth, Margaret and Lady Anne play in political life.

4 Examine Queen Margaret's function in this scene.

Beyond the text

5 Writing In the scene, the quarrel between the Woodvilles and Richard takes up much space. Equally, Margaret's accusations and curses are presented in great detail. Imagine you are William Shakespeare and a censor demands that you cut out these passages. Write a letter justifying your decision to include so much of the two families' backstory.

6 In some theatre performances, Margaret's part has been cut out altogether. With a partner, discuss what is lost if she does not appear.

B5 The killers (Act I, Scene 4, from l. 162)

In his prison cell in the Tower, Clarence tells his jailer about the nightmare he has just had: his brother Richard accidentally threw him overboard from a ship. Drowning, Clarence saw the men he had killed in war accusing him of his deeds. He is greatly shaken by this. When two new guards take over, he is asleep again. They are actually assassins sent by Richard who discuss how to kill Clarence.

Read Scene 4 from the moment Clarence wakes up (cf. l. 162).

Comprehension

1 Correct the mistakes in the following text.

A Clarence claims it was his brother Edward who killed the former king's son.

____

B Clarence curses Richard for seeking his death.

____

C Clarence thinks that both assassins are keen on killing him.

____

D The two murderers drown Clarence in a butt of Malmsey wine.

____

Analysis

2 Analyse the way the themes of sinning and remorse are treated in this scene.

Beyond the text

3 In this scene, the fatal consequences of Richard's villainy are shown on stage. Discuss what effect the murder of Clarence might have on the audience.

B6 Looking back on Act I

1 Write the names of the noble characters you have met so far (living or dead) in the correct place in the table below.

The House of York	The House of Lancaster
______________________	______________________
______________________	______________________
______________________	______________________

Woodvilles	Other noblemen
______________________	______________________
______________________	______________________
______________________	______________________
	______________________

Buckingham
Catesby
Clarence
Dead King Henry VI
Dead Prince Edward
Derby
Dorset
Hastings
Margaret
King Edward IV
Queen Elizabeth
Richard
Rivers

2 Watch the first ten minutes of the film *Richard III*. With your knowledge of Act I, Scenes 1 + 3 in mind, comment on the effectiveness of the cinematic devices chosen by the film director.

B7 Overview: Act II and Act III, Scenes 1–3

Act II

Expecting his imminent death, King Edward IV urges the opposing parts of his family to cooperate. Everyone including Richard vows they will be reconciled. Richard informs the king that Clarence is dead, pretending he was executed in accordance with the king's death sentence. Since Edward had reversed the sentence of death, he is extremely upset and fears God's punishment for his seeming lack of mercy. Richard uses the opportunity to again blame the queen and the Woodvilles for Clarence's death.
When King Edward dies, Earl Rivers urges his sister, Queen Elizabeth, not to waste time grieving, but to crown her eldest son quickly in order to keep the Woodvilles in power. When Richard and Buckingham arrive to offer their condolences, the latter suggests that the young prince (now Edward V) be taken to London for his coronation by an escort. When alone, the two men decide to separate the prince from the Woodvilles.

Queen Elizabeth and her youngest son, the Duke of York, the Archbishop of York and the Duchess of York are waiting for the prince's arrival in London. The Duchess (i. e. Richard's, Clarence's and King Edward's mother) feels great sorrow for the loss of her two sons. A messenger arrives with bad news: Richard and Buckingham have sent three members of the Woodville family to Pomfret Castle, a place known for executions. Elizabeth foresees the ruin of her house and with her young son seeks sanctuary in a church.

Act III, Scenes 1–3

Richard, Buckingham, the Archbishop of Canterbury (who traditionally crowns the king) and the Mayor of London welcome Prince Edward to London, who is surprised not to find his family there. Urged on by Richard, the Archbishop agrees to fetch Edward's brother, the young Duke of York, from his sanctuary. Richard admonishes the princes to stay at the Tower (both a castle and a prison) for their own safety, which they reluctantly agree to. Buckingham sends Catesby to sound Hastings out about his possible support for their plot to gain the crown and conspires further with Richard, who promises Buckingham the Earldom of Hereford. Lord Hastings, the Lord Chamberlain, is glad to hear that his opponents from the Woodville family will meet their deaths. However, he will not support Richard's bid for the crown and has publicly declared he will be loyal to King Edward's heir. When Derby, generally mistrustful of Richard, has even more misgivings about Richard's intentions because of an ominous dream, Hastings dismisses such worries and claims that Richard poses no threat.

B8 The manipulator (Act III, Scene 4)

Read Scene 4.

Comprehension

1 Divide the dialogue into sense units which match the headings in the table below. Number the headings in the correct chronological order and add the line numbers in the column on the right.

Headings	Order	Lines
A Avoiding eavesdroppers	____________	____________
B A lack of foresight	____________	____________
C Finding the royal day	____________	____________
D A monstrous accusation	____________	____________
E Arriving late	____________	____________
F Judging Richard's mood	____________	____________

2 Reread the summary of Act III, Scenes 1–3 on p. 122. Use the information given there and the passage where Hastings expresses his regrets (cf. Scene 4, ll. 80–107). Outline the mistakes he has made for which he will pay with his life.

Analysis

3 Illustrate how Shakespeare creates an atmosphere (→ Info box, p. 160) of evil and doom in this scene. Examine the effect this has on how Richard is seen by the audience.

Language help
evoke / conjure up / convey an atmosphere of … • create / establ sh a mood of … • the scene is charged with / pervaded by … • the choice of words conveys … • references to … add to the mood of … • have connotations of …

Beyond the text

4 **Speaking** A student plays Hastings and slowly walks between two rows of students facing each other. They tell Hastings what he should have done.

B9 The plotter (Act III, Scene 5, from l. 72)

In the courtyard of the Tower, Richard and Buckingham meet the Mayor of London and convince him that Hastings is a traitor who tried to kill them both and therefore deserves his death.

Read Scene 5 (from l. 72).

Comprehension

1 Tick the correct answer.

a Richard tells Buckingham to …

A stop the Mayor before he can reach London.
B get to the town hall before the appointed time.
C follow the Mayor to the town hall.

lines: ____________

b He asks him to spread rumours about the late king, saying that . .

A he had an extravagant lifestyle.
B he took every chance to find sexual pleasure.
C he promised to make his son heir to the crown.

lines: ____________

c Buckingham should also say that …

A Richard's mother was unfaithful to her husband. **B** Richard's father was away at war when Edward was born. **C** Richard's brother looks very much like their father.	lines: ________________

d Richard's next plans are to …

A ask two churchmen for their assistance. **B** wait for news from the town hall. **C** isolate the royal children for his own purposes.	lines: ________________

Beyond the text

2 Writing When Buckingham meets the Mayor and does as Richard told him, a reporter from a tabloid newspaper overhears their conversation. Write his or her article using a fitting style to express what Richard wants the public to know.

B10 The actor (Act III, Scene 7)

Buckingham has not been able to convince the Londoners to see Richard as their new king. He suggests that Richard make a carefully staged appearance before the Mayor of London and a crowd of citizens.

Watch Scene 7 of the film *Richard III* (00:59:36–01:03:40).

Richard III statue in Leicester

Comprehension

1 Viewing Watch the segment of the film *Richard III* from 00:59:36–01:03:40. Describe which strategies Richard and Buckingham employ to convince the audience that he is the ideal king.

Analysis

2 Viewing Watch the segment of the film in which the crowd cheer for Richard in an auditorium (01:02:07–01:03:40). Analyse the cinematic devices used and the effect they create.

Beyond the text

3 Read the part of Scene 7 that matches the film adaptation (ll. 94–246). Compare the two versions with regard to the action, the characters and the setting of Richard's ultimate triumph.

B11 Looking back on Acts II and III

1 **Writing** Write Buckingham's to-do list in which he notes down all the steps of his strategy to make Richard king.
2 Richard is a brilliant actor who can fool others into believing what he tells them. Design a mind map with Richard in the centre bubble and the different roles he has played so far in the connecting bubbles.
3 Shakespeare has included very short scenes with minor characters in these two acts. They show London citizens worrying about the king-to-be (Act II, Scene 3), a scrivener criticizing the injustice of Hastings's death (Act III, Scene 6) or the Woodville men on their way to their executions commenting on Richard's unscrupulous scheming (Act III, Scene 3). Explain the functions these scenes might fulfil in the play.

B12 The usurper (Act IV, Scene 1, from l. 28)

The Duchess of York, Queen Elizabeth and her son Dorset want to pay the princes a visit in the Tower. Lady Anne, now Richard's wife, has come with the same intention, but they are all barred from seeing the boys. The women are outraged and demand entry, but are rejected.

Read Scene 1 (from l. 28).

Comprehension

1 Sum up …
   a the news that Derby brings.
   b the women's reactions to the news.
2 Identify the lines in which …
   a Queen Elizabeth warns that Dorset is in mortal danger and says that she has no hard feelings towards Anne.
   b Anne admits that she was seduced by Richard's way with words and foresees her own death at his hands.

Analysis

3 Point out the means used by Shakespeare to turn the harmonious atmosphere to despair.

Beyond the text

4 Imagine the women were your contemporaries and not bound by Elizabethan laws and customs, which practically made them their father's or husband's property.
   a **Think:** Imagine what each woman could do today to change her situation.
   b **Pair:** Exchange views with a partner. Agree on the two best ideas.
   c **Speaking** **Share:** Work with another pair to discuss your views. Again decide on the two best ideas and present them to the class.

B13 The troubled king (Act IV, Scene 2)

Read Scene 2.

Comprehension

1 **Writing** Richard's henchman Ratcliffe overhears everything that is said in this scene. Write a string of tweets (240 characters each) to share the latest news with his followers.

Analysis

2 Despite just having seized the throne, Richard feels insecure about his reign. Examine the means Shakespeare uses to convey his state of mind.

Beyond the text

3 **Hot seat:** Full of resentment, Buckingham leaves London to return to his Welsh estate and raise an army against Richard. He tries to convince two other lords to join his enterprise with their men.
Work in groups of three to prepare a hot seat activity with Buckingham in the middle and the other lords asking him probing questions (e.g. why he supported Richard in the first place, if they can trust him now). Make sure Buckingham replies honestly without hiding his feelings towards Richard.

- **a** As one of the lords, prepare questions to ask Buckingham. As Buckingham, imagine what questions you might be asked and how to answer them.
- **b** **Speaking** Carry out the hot seat activity.

B14 Overview: Act IV, Scene 3

In a monologue, Tyrell reveals that two helpers have murdered the princes and felt great remorse afterwards. To Richard, however, he simply reports the job done and is promised a reward. In the meantime, Anne has died and Clarence's children are disposed of. When Catesby informs Richard that Buckingham is gathering troops against him and that the Bishop of Exeter now supports Richmond, Richard makes plans to marry King Edward's daughter, Elizabeth York, as soon as possible to prevent Richmond from doing it first. Even though the loss of followers has weakened him considerably, Richard prepares for battle.

B15 Object of hatred (Act IV, Scene 4, up to l. 196)

Read Scene 4 up to l. 196.

Comprehension

1 Summarize the dialogue of the three queens.

Analysis

2 Examine the relationships of the three queens and the function of their laments.

3 Analyse the way Richard, Elizabeth and his mother speak to each other (cf. ll. 36–196).

Beyond the text

4 **Writing** Choose one of the three widows and write her interior monologue (→ Info box, p. 173), expressing her feelings at this moment and describing the resolutions she has made for the future.

5 Elizabethans believed that physical deformities were caused by a person's inner evil. Modern psychology claims that a mother's hostile attitude towards her child will influence its character development negatively.

- **a** **Speaking** With a partner, re-read the abuses directed at Richard by Anne (cf. ll. 2, 102), Margaret (cf. l. 3), Elizabeth (cf. l. 81) and his mother (cf. ll. 163–196) and say them out loud.
- **b** Compare the women's descriptions to what Richard says about himself in Act I, Scene 1, ll. 16–23.
- **c** Interpret Richard's reactions to his mother's words (cf. ll. 137–196). Assess whether her attitude towards him might have had an influence on his personality.

6 As a director of a film or a theatrical performance, how would you present Richard's deformity?

B16 Pure evil (Act IV, Scene 4, ll. 197–430)

Watch part of the scene from the film (01:18:40–01:22:48).

Comprehension

1 **Listening** Tick the arguments Richard gives to make Elizabeth persuade her daughter to marry him.

A Queen Elizabeth will be the mother of a king.
B The princess will be able to live a life of luxury and abundance.
C The princess would not have to live with Richard.
D Princess Elizabeth will marry a powerful man who has defeated his enemies.
E Princess Elizabeth will make him happy.
F Both women ought to consider his future deeds rather than the ones of the past.
G Queen Elizabeth's dead sons will live on in the children Princess Elizabeth will bear.

Analysis

2 Read ll. 406–419, a part of the scene you've just watched. Analyse the means Richard employs to persuade Elizabeth. Pay special attention to his choice of words.

Beyond the text

3 Comment on Richard's marriage proposal to his own niece in view of the crimes he has already committed against his family.

4 Compare this scene to Richard's wooing of Lady Anne in Act I, Scene 2.

Making predictions

5 When Elizabeth has left, Richard calls her 'Relenting fool, and shallow, changing woman' (cf. l. 431). Discuss whether you also think Elizabeth will agree to Richard's plan.

B17 Under pressure (Act IV, Scene 4, from l. 433)

Read the rest of the scene.

Comprehension

1 In modern English, write short dialogues containing the news that are brought to Richard and his reactions to them. You could start like this:

> **Ratcliffe:** My good lord, there's a powerful navy arriving on the western coast.
> **Richard:** …

Analysis

2 Analyse how suspense is created in this passage.

Beyond the text

3 Work in groups of four and prepare to perform parts of your dialogues from **1** in front of the class. Your teacher will assign one of the following passages to you:
- Richard, Ratcliffe and Catesby
- Richard, Ratcliffe and Derby or
- Richard, Ratcliffe and Messenger 1/2/3/4

a In your group, decide who is going to be the director and who is going to play one of the roles, then prepare and practice your passages.

b **Speaking** Show the individual scenes to the class.

c Discuss how they can be strung together into a suspenseful theatrical experience.

d **Speaking** Rehearse again and perform the whole scene with a special focus on how the increasing pressure takes its toll on Richard.

B18 Overview: Act IV, Scene 5

Derby sends a messenger to his stepson Richmond. He tells him that he can't openly side with him because Richard holds his, Derby's, son George hostage to ensure Derby's loyalty. Elizabeth wants Richmond to know that she agrees to him marrying her daughter Elizabeth. Meanwhile, Richmond's army has arrived in Wales, where many more noblemen have embraced his cause.

B19 Looking back on Act IV

1 Explain the role children play in this drama.
2 Discuss Richard's relationships with women.
3 Richard's schemes have had severe consequences for most characters. Write the names of the following characters in the table below to indicate where they are now.

King Edward IV
the princes
Richmond
Vaughan
Princess Elizabeth
Edward, King Henry's son
Anne
Clarence
Margaret
Hastings
Dorset
Elizabeth
King Henry VI
Buckingham (arrested)
Rivers
Grey
Derby

A	B	C	D	E
				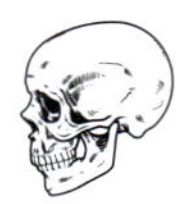
Ready to fight Richard	Secretly scheming	In exile	In a sanctuary	Dead

B20 King under threat (Act V, Scenes 1–3)

Read Act V, Scenes 1–3.

Comprehension

1 Complete the following sentences.

A When Buckingham imagines that the souls of Richard's victims might be seeing him,

he begs them to ____.

B Buckingham finds his punishment __________________________________.

C Richmond has received a report from Derby saying that ____________________

____.

D Richmond's followers are convinced that _____________________________

____.

E Richard gives orders to (1) ____________________________________,

(2) ____ and

(3) ____.

F He is confident to win because (1) ________________________________

____ and

(2) ____

____.

Analysis

2 Richmond, the hero of the play, appears very late in the drama.

- **a** With a partner, collect information the audience has got about Richmond before he enters the scene. It may be helpful to have another look at Act IV, Scene 2.
- **b** Examine the means Shakespeare uses to create a positive impression of Richmond in Act V, Scene 2 and before.

3 Richard's heraldic symbol is the white boar, and Richmond uses a boar to describe Richard (cf. Act V, Scene 2, ll. 7–11). Analyse this metaphor and point out why Richard's emblem fits him well or not.

Beyond the text

4 Re-read Margaret's prophecies in Act I, Scene 3, ll. 186–301. Explain which ones have been fulfilled and which haven't.

5 **Writing** Before the execution, Buckingham is allowed to write a farewell letter to his family. Write his letter, explaining how the political events have influenced his life and led to his imminent death. Add advice on how his children should deal with rulers. Make sure to decide beforehand whether Buckingham's remorse is heartfelt.

6 Imagine Buckingham was allowed to speak to King Richard.

a **Writing** With a partner, write a short scene about Buckingham and Richard's encounter. Include a moment of high tension and a dramatic ending. Make sure to keep their present attitudes to their actions in mind.

b **Speaking** Rehearse and perform your scene.

B21 The soul-searcher (Act V, Scene 4)

Read Scene 4.

Comprehension

1 Divide the dialogue into units which match the headings in the table below. Number the headings in the correct chronological order and add the line numbers in the column on the right.

Headings	Order	Lines
A A pep talk	______	______
B The messenger	______	______
C Soul-searching and torment	______	______
D Richard's preparation for battle	______	______
E A parade of apparitions	______	______
F Richmond's military consultation	______	______
G Praying for victory	______	______

Analysis

2 Analyse how language is used to illustrate the affection between Derby and his stepson Richmond (cf. ll. 59–87).

3 Examine in what ways Richard's monologue (cf. ll. 158–186) differs from earlier ones.

Language help
tremble with fear · have pangs of conscience · be deeply troubled by sb./sth. · pity sb. · speak measured lines · straightforward argument · weigh your words · jump from one thought to another · be agitated · feel undisguised glee · self-analysis · stick to sth.

Beyond the text

4 Assess whether Richard's inner turmoil reveals true remorse.

5 Discuss what message Shakespeare might have wanted to convey with the parade of ghosts.

6 **Writing** Imagine you are a theatre director. You want to stage the ghosts' appearance and their movement between the two camps. Write stage directions.

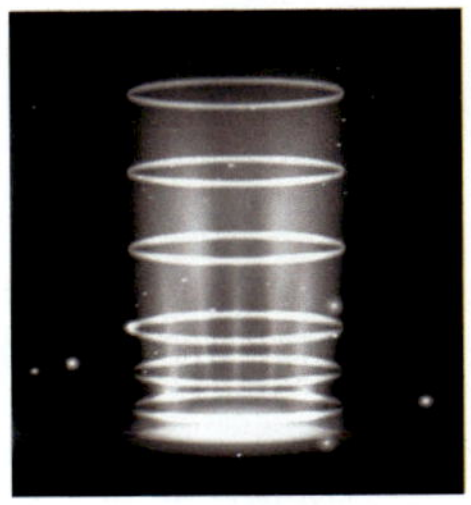

7 Imagine you are a movie director. With a partner, exchange ideas on the cinematic effects you would use to establish the supernatural.

8 **Viewing** Watch the extract from the film *Richard III* in which Richard's nightmare and his reaction to it are shown (1:28:45–1:31:10). Compare it to the drama (cf. ll. 98–202).

B22 The orator (Act V, Scene 5)

Read Scene 5.

Comprehension

1 Imagine you are a war correspondent reporting back to your editor in London about the preparations for battle. Write your text messages summarizing what you can observe.

Scene from the 2003 re-enactment of the Battle of Bosworth Field, the last battle of the Wars of the Roses

Analysis

2 Compare the language and rhetorical devices used by Richard (cf. ll. 43–70) and Richmond (cf. Act V, Scene 4, ll. 216–250) in their speeches to their soldiers.

Beyond the text

3 Discuss for what reasons (apart from the one given in the scene) George Stanley is not executed when his father Derby refuses to join Richard's troops.

B23 The defeated king (Act V, Scenes 6 and 7)

Read Scenes 6 and 7.

Comprehension

1 Mark the sentences as true or false. Correct the wrong ones.

	True	False	Correction
A Richard has outdone himself fighting against his enemies.			___
B Richard is looking for his white horse Surrey.			___
C Derby puts the crown on Richmond's head.			___
D Richmond announces that Richard's soldiers will not face punishment if they surrender.			___
E Richmond announces the union of the Houses of Lancaster and York, brought about by his marriage to Elizabeth York.			___

Analysis

2 Analyse how Richard's keen fighting spirit and physical power are underlined in Scene 6.

Beyond the text

3 a **Speaking** Find different ways of saying Richard's most famous sentence: 'A horse! A horse! My kingdom for a horse!' (cf. Scene 6, ll. 8 and 14). You could e.g. be cool, whining, barking an order or promising a great reward. Present your versions to the class and decide which ones are most convincing.

b **Speaking** One student says Richard's sentence while all others stand behind him or her. After a second, each one in the group expresses the emotions or thoughts that are running through their heads (e.g. 'I could still desert right now', 'Our king needs my help', 'Where is a horse?'). Perform the sequence three times, with Richard expressing the phrase in a different manner each time.

4 a Work with a partner and discuss how you would present the two following situations in a freeze frame:
- Richard receiving the deadly hit from Richmond in battle
- Richmond's speech to the soldiers.

Assign a role to each student.

b Present the freeze frames to class.

c After seeing a few freeze frames, discuss which rendition you found most convincing. Say why.

B24 Looking back at the drama

1 Compare Richard's and Richmond's leadership qualities in their fight for the throne.

2 Using the information from the info box below, fill in the table to indicate where the elements of drama are to be found in the play.

Element	in *Richard III*
Exposition	
Inciting moment	
Rising action	
Turning point	
Falling action	
Resolution	

Info Dramatic structure
Shakespeare's plays are divided into five distinctive sections. The action starts with the **exposition** (→ Info box, p. 95), which introduces the protagonists and the main plot. It is then driven forward by the **inciting moment**, i. e. an event which leads to a problem that needs to be solved during the play. Further conflicts complicate the plot and the characters encounter more obstacles in the next phase, the **rising action**. The highest point of tension is reached with the **turning point**, which marks a complete change for the protagonist for better or worse. The following phase is called the **falling action**. It contains developments leading to the **resolution** that ends the play.

Part C
Post-reading activities

C1 Themes

1 a In groups, choose one of the major themes from *Richard III* below and examine what role it plays in the drama.

ambition · disability · rejection · sibling rivalry · fear · family conflict · jealousy · loyalty · deception · women and children · justice and punishment · sin and atonement · appearance and reality

b **Speaking** Give a short presentation of your findings to the class.
c Say which theme(s) you personally find most relevant for the play. Give reasons.
d Illustrate your chosen theme(s) in a collage.

C2 Richard's relationships

1 No dictator or tyrant can operate in a vacuum. On the contrary, they need supporters at their side and/or they have to deal with opponents who seek their own profit. Assess the motives of some courtiers (e.g. Hastings, the Woodvilles) and those of Richard's entourage (e.g. Buckingham, Tyrell).

2 Richard's antagonist, the Earl of Richmond (later King Henry VII), represents the force of good, which finally conquers Richard's force of evil. Discuss what Shakespeare's dramatic intention might have been in letting Richard be so dominant in the play. Use the expressions in the box below.

Language help
rise in revolt · ascend to the throne · seize [siːz] the crown · reign of terror · restore the divine order · tyrannical regime [tɪˈrænɪkl reɪˈʒiːm] · contender for the throne · successor · lineal heir [eə] to the throne · predecessor · cow sb. into submission · all-conquering hero · usurper [juːˈzɜːpə]

C3 The real Richard?

1 Niccolò Machiavelli (1469–1527), an Italian statesman, suggested in his book *Il Principe* (*The Prince*, 1513) that it is acceptable for a ruler to use deceit and to murder people for effective policy-making.

a Discuss the morality of Machiavelli's principles.

b Compare the political power plays of modern politicians with those of Shakespeare's *Richard III*.

2 **Hot seat**: Work in groups to prepare a hot seat activity in which you put Shakespeare in the hot seat and ask him:
- why he presented Richard as a self-centred villain
- why he didn't stick to a historically true portrait of King Richard III.

Go back to your findings from **A3** (cf. p. 113).

a Prepare further questions you could ask Shakespeare or answers you could give to the questions, depending on your role.

b **Speaking** Carry out the activity.

Statue of Niccolò Machiavelli in Florence, Italy

C4 Relationships

1 After reading the excerpts from *Richard III*, complete a relationship map for the main characters of the drama from below. Indicate family relations, emotional attitudes and vital deeds (e.g. 'mother to', 'hates', 'orders his death', etc.).

King Henry VI

Lady Anne

Clarence

Duchess of York

Prince Edward

Queen Elizabeth

Queen Margaret

King Edward IV

two princes

Richmond

Richard

Princess Elizabeth

Module IV

Mother to Mother

Part A
Pre-reading activities

A1 Working with words

One of the major topics of the novel *Mother to Mother* is dealing with crime and injustice.

1 Look at the following word bank and make sure you understand all the words. If necessary, check the meanings in a dictionary. You can also arrange the words and ideas in a mind map.

reconciliation · prison · jail · (to) convict · consequences · prospects · (to) come to terms with sth. · legitimate · legal · unjust · oppression · inferior · superior · remorse · guilty conscience · (to) come clean · (to) commit a crime · confession · (to) resolve a crime · trial · (to) resist · amnesty · equal rights · (to) get away with (a crime) · (to) serve time in prison · forgiveness · (to) negotiate · living conditions · an eye for an eye · conflict · responsibility · education · redemption · atonement · (to) turn a blind eye to sth. · a (criminal) case · (to) charge sb. · shame · violence · injustice · (to) protest · (to) cope with sth. · (to) struggle with sth.

2 Work with a partner and talk about crime. Try to use as many of the words in the box as possible.
- **a** Why do you think people commit crimes?
- **b** List some crimes and discuss who is responsible. Sometimes the answer is more complex than it seems at first glance.
- **c** What legal and personal consequences do crimes have for perpetrators and victims?
- **d** What can governments and societies do to reduce crime?

A2 Understanding the background

1 a Form five groups. Each group does some research on one of the following topics. Prepare a presentation for your class.

A Grand apartheid

B Petty apartheid; Bantu Education

C Mandela and de Klerk: The peaceful transition from 1990–1994

D Life in Guguletu, a township outside Cape Town

E The Truth and Reconciliation Commission; the Norgaard principles

b **Speaking** Give your presentation to your class. Take short notes during the other groups' presentations.

A3 The author

Info Dr Sindiwe Magona

Dr Sindiwe Magona (*23 August, 1943) is a South African writer and women's rights activist.
Born in South Africa, she graduated from Columbia University in 1981 and spent more than 20 years in New York, working for the United Nations. After her retirement in 2003, she returned to Cape Town. Many of her publications have been influenced by her experience of suffering under apartheid and poverty.
For her outstanding literary and academic achievements as well as for her humanitarian efforts, Magona has received many awards, including an honorary doctorate from Harwick College in 1993 and the Order of Ikhamanga in 2011.

1 **Speaking** Use the internet to find out more about Sindiwe Magona's life under apartheid and the hardships she faced as a young woman. Present your findings to your class.

Part B
While-reading activities

B1 A timeline

1 In the novel *Mother to Mother* Sindiwe Magona has chosen a narrative technique that uses different time layers which re-occur in many chapters. In order to understand all the important events, create a timeline and add information while reading the novel.

1968:
At the age of nine, Mandisa is forced to move to Guguletu

1972:
...

B2 Character profiles

1 Start character profiles for the major characters of the novel and add information while you read. Write down relevant page numbers and/or highlight interesting quotes.

a Mandisa
b Mxolisi
c The white girl

B3 Mandisa's lament (chapter 1)

Comprehension

1 Read chapter 1 and finish the sentences below.

A Mandisa writes a letter to ______________________________

______________________________.

B Her son has killed a ______________________________

______________________________.

C She says that children in Guguletu have become ______________________________

____.

D She accuses the victim of ______________________________

____.

E The white girl has come to Africa to ______________________________

____.

F Mandisa says that when a white girl is killed, it is a big issue but if a black person dies,

____.

G In prison, her son gets ______________________________

____.

H Mandisa works as a ______________________________ and

has no time for ______________________________.

I She asks ______________________________ for forgiveness for her son's crime.

Analysis

2 Work with a partner and answer the questions below.

- **a** Explain the title of the novel *Mother to Mother*.
- **b** Explain what we learn about Mandisa and her son Mxolisi in chapter 1.
- **c** Examine the atmosphere in chapter 1 (→ Info box, p. 160).
- **d** Outline Mandisa's criticism of the white girl's behaviour.
- **e** Examine to what extent Mandisa blames Guguletu and the government for the murder.

Language help

tense · shocked · sad · reflective · melancholy · lonely · angry · sensible · desperate · pessimistic · nightmarish · gloomy · hopeless · sympathetic · exhausted · conciliatory · doubtful · concerned · respectful · straightforward · frustrated · naïve

Beyond the text

3 **Speaking** Imagine you are the victim's mother. Discuss the letter in chapter 1 with your husband.

B4 Life in Guguletu (chapter 2)

Look at the picture.

Township in South Africa

1 a Think: Imagine you live in one of the shacks in the picture above. What do you think about your life there? Write down your thoughts in a speech bubble.

b Speaking **Pair:** Compare your results with a partner.

c Speaking **Share:** Find another pair and present your speech bubbles to each other.

Comprehension

2 Read chapter 2 and tick the correct answer in the table below. Only one option is correct.

a Mandisa …

A works for Mr Nelson in a factory at the Cape Town docks.
B has lost her job.
C works full time as a housemaid and still hardly gets by.
D is a waitress in a local café.

b The white girl …

A is about to fly back home to the USA after 10 months of studying in South Africa.
B has just arrived in South Africa and is going to study there for the next 10 months.
C has returned to South Africa as a tourist.
D is still in the USA and about to leave for South Africa.

c Children in Guguletu …

A go to school but protest against their white teachers.
B take the bus to attend better schools in Cape Town's wealthy districts.
C refuse to go to school and go on 'strike'.
D study at home because they reject the school system.

d The white girl …

- **A** takes her black friends home in her car.
- **B** is on her way to the airport.
- **C** is not accepted by black students at her university.
- **D** has joined the protests against the education system.

e When a car enters Guguletu to deliver drugs to a black tuberculosis clinic, …

- **A** people welcome the help but yell at the white driver.
- **B** it is escorted to the clinic in order to protect the driver from the angry mob.
- **C** the black driver is dragged out of the car and stabbed.
- **D** it is burned as the rioters do not accept any help sent by whites.

3 Work with a partner.
a Find 3 suitable adjectives to describe life in the township as portrayed in chapter 2.
b Join another pair and compare your words.
4 Describe the white girl's life in South Africa.

Analysis

5 Read the info box below and examine the way students protest in chapter 2.
6 Examine the role of the police as described on pp. 16–18.

Info COSAS

The Congress of South African Students (COSAS) is a students' movement, which was established in 1979 to protest the racist South African education system. Students were most active in the 1980s when they used strikes and boycotts to draw attention to their cause. Sometimes, these demonstrations became out of control with angry crowds attacking everything they regarded as a symbol of the despised apartheid government. COSAS is still campaigning for students' rights and a fair education system.

Beyond the text

7 **Writing** Choose one of the following writing assignments.
a Write a newspaper report about the COSAS riots in chapter 2 from the point of view of a neutral observer (third-person narrator, → Info box, p. 29).
OR
b Write Mxolisi's diary entry after taking part in the 'strike'.

B5 Ethnic diversity: The lives of black and white South Africans (chapters 3–4)

Comprehension

1 Read chapters 3 and 4 and match the following sentence halves.

A On Wednesday, Mrs Nelson takes her

B Guguletu means

C According to Mandisa, the police are

D The township of Guguletu is described as

E In 1968, people are forced

F Arriving in Guguletu, they

G Being displaced by the government

H Mandisa learns from her neighbour that

I Rapes, murders and assaults are

J Mrs Nelson drives Mandisa to the station because she has heard about trouble in Guguletu. Mandisa

1 'our pride', which is odd as no one can be proud of a place like this.

2 criminals themselves.

3 poor and dirty with littered streets and congested shacks.

4 common in Guguletu. That is why Mandisa fears for her daughter's safety.

5 students often cannot be admitted to school, or refuse to go there as they do not learn anything useful anyway.

6 a white girl has been stabbed in her district of Guguletu.

7 fears that her children could be involved in the riots.

8 do not have enough houses and many people must build shacks out of any material they can find.

9 'day off' although she hardly works at all.

10 to move to Guguletu where they live among strangers, with their communities being ripped apart.

Analysis

2 Divide the class into two groups. Each of you works on one of the following assignments.
  - **a** Examine Mrs. Nelson's life.
  - **b** Examine the life of blacks in Guguletu.
  - **c** Find a partner from the other group and compare your results. Take short notes.

3 Together with a partner, discuss the three most pressing issues in Guguletu. Compare your list with another pair and agree on a ranking.

Beyond the text

4 Work with a partner. Choose one of the statistics below that depict poverty and inequality in South Africa. Present your data to your partner and then discuss to what extent the situation in South Africa has changed since apartheid.

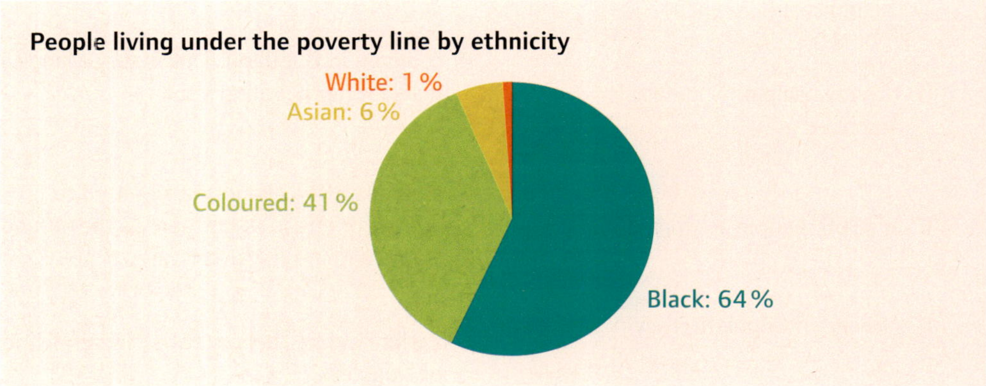

Data from: Stats SA's Poverty Trends in South Africa (2015)

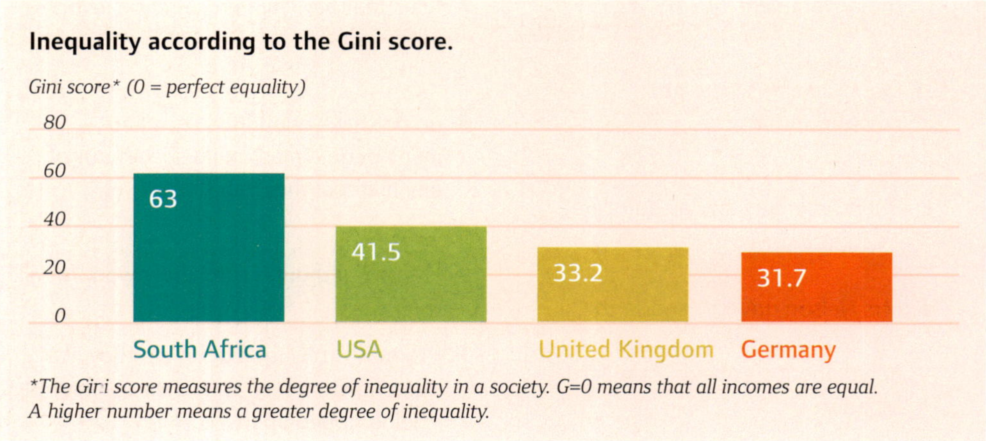

Data from: World Bank, Development Research Group. Data are based on primary household survey data obtained from government statistical agencies and World Bank country departments.

B6 Grand apartheid is enforced (chapters 5–6)

1 a Read again what you have learned about grand apartheid (**A2**, p. 138).
b **Speaking** Prepare a one-minute presentation for your partner.

Comprehension

2 Read chapters 5 and 6. Quickly scan the text for specific information. Use short answers only.

A Where does Mandisa live at the age of 9? ______________________

B What does the leaflet dropped by the plane tell people to do? (p. 59) ______________________

____

C Where does Mandisa's father work? (p. 63) ______________________

____

D Who do the desperate people appeal to for help? (p. 63) ______________________

____

E When are they going to be relocated by the government? (p. 63) ______________________

____

F How are people forced out of their houses? (p. 65) ______________________

____

G What jobs do most black women do once they have arrived in the townships? (p. 67) ______

____

H What is Siziwe's father's name? ______________________

____

I According to Mandisa, why was the white girl killed? (p. 69) ______________________

____

J What happens to the three white activists trying to protect blacks from police violence in 1960? ______________________

K What sound do you often hear in Guguletu at night? (p. 70) ______________________________

____

L How old is Mxolisi and in which year is he at school? (p. 72) ______________________________

____

M What do the rioting youths call themselves and who supports them? (pp. 75–76) __________

____

N What terrible crime is described on pp. 77–78? ______________________________

____

O Who saves a girl from being raped? (p. 80) ______________________________

____

P Who does Mandisa fear most? (p. 82)? ______________________________

____

Q Who is beaten up at 4 a. m.? (p. 87) ______________________________

____

3 Describe the community's reaction to the leaflet.
4 Describe the forced removal of blacks from their homes.

Analysis

5 Using the information from chapter 5, compare Mandisa's idyllic childhood life in Blouvlei with life in Guguletu.
6 Examine the role of the police.

Beyond the text

7 Writing Choose **a** or **b**.

a Imagine you are a police officer. Write your diary entry the day after you moved the black community to Guguletu.
OR
b Choose a situation during the forced relocation (pp. 54–67) and write Mandisa's interior monologue (→ Info box, p. 173).

B7 Teenage pregnancy (chapter 7)

1 Describe the cartoon and explain its message. Assess to what extent common stereotypes – as depicted in the cartoon – are accurate or rather insulting.

2 Using the following quote and the cartoon as a starting point, discuss the role of teenage pregnancies in our society today.

> *'You are supposed to be changing the world … Not changing diapers.'*

"I wanted to be a barrister or solicitor but now I want to be a burden on society."

Comprehension

3 Fill in the gaps with information from chapter 7.

A Mandisa's friend, ______________________________, becomes Khaya's lover. (p. 89)

B Mandisa has a boyfriend, ______________________________.

Her mum is worried she could get ______________________________.

She holds a high position at ______________________________. (p. 94)

C Mandisa's schoolmate, Ribba, dies in an ______________________________. (p. 95)

D The Ntloko family learns that Nono ______________________________. (p. 97)

E To prevent Mandisa from getting pregnant, her parents send her to ______________

______________________________. (p. 99)

F Mandisa is a very ______________________________ student. (p. 107)

G Although being a confirmed virgin, Mandisa ______________________________ at the age of 13.

4 Describe what measures Mandisa's parents take to prevent a teenage pregnancy.

Analysis

5 Explain the role of education in Mandisa's life and how her pregnancy is going to affect her plans.

Beyond the text

6 **Speaking** Choose one of the following situations and act out a dialogue with a partner. Take the following aspects into consideration: Mrs. Ntloko's position at the church, Mandisa's education, a possible wedding with China, child care and financial troubles.

a Mandisa talks to her mother about her pregnancy.
OR

b Mandisa's parents discuss how to deal with Mandisa's pregnancy.

7 **Writing** Write Mandisa's diary entry after the conversation with her mother.

8 What would Mandisa think if she saw the cartoon above? Write a few sentences summing up her possible reaction to it.

B8 Growing up in Guguletu (chapter 8)

Comprehension

1 Read chapter 8 and put the following sentences into the right order. Write the numbers 1–12 on the lines after each sentence.

A After Mxolisi's second birthday, China leaves the family. ________

B Mandisa meets Lungile and has her second child, Lunga. ________

C At their clans' insistence, Mandisa and China get married without a proper celebration. ________

D Mxolisi saves a girl from being raped and becomes a community hero. ________

E China works at a meat storage facility to provide for his young family. He blames Mandisa for not having had an abortion. ________

F Mandisa has to care for her baby and her unwelcoming in-laws who do not let her go back to school. ________

G Mxolisi quits school and joins the angry gangs on the street. ________

H At the age of four, Mxolisi witnesses the police shooting his teenage friends, Mzama and Zazi. As a result, he stops talking for two years. ________

I When Mxolisi wets his bed, his stepfather, Lungile, makes him eat a mouse, which shocks him out of his muteness. ________

J China's family decides to name his baby Mxolisi, 'He who brings peace'. ________

K Mandisa marries Dwadwa and has her third child, Siziwe. ________

L Their child is born on 4th January, 1973. ________

Analysis

2 Examine Mxolisi's life from his birth to becoming a community hero as a young adult and add your findings to his character profile (**B2**, p. 139).

- **a** Write down your results. Use short notes only.
- **b** Compare your list with a partner and add any missing aspects.

3 Illustrate how the pregnancy and the living conditions in the township affect Mandisa's and Mxolisi's lives and her feelings toward her son.

4 Explain the meaning of the angry slogan 'One settler, one bullet'.

Beyond the text

5 In a group of four, discuss how both Mandisa's and Mxolisi's lives would be different if they were white. Would poverty and the teenage pregnancy have a similar impact on their lives?

B9 Looking for the murderer (chapters 9–10)

Comprehension

1 Read chapters 9 and 10 and find out who the missing people are.

A The ________________________________ are looking for Mxolisi.

B ____________________ and Dwadwa are badly bruised from the police raid.

C ________________ tells Mandisa that Mxolisi has been home to hide something.

D ______________________________'s room is destroyed by the police.

E ___________________________ sends Mandisa out to look for Mxolisi.

F Mandisa finds ________________ in a deserted house where they hug and cry.

G ______________ illustrates how the angry mob and 'a knife' killed the white girl.

Analysis

2 Illustrate how, according to Mandisa's grandfather, blacks have got into the desperate situation they find themselves in today.

Beyond the text

3 **Writing** Focus on the day when the police search for Mxolisi and Mandisa finally finds him in hiding. Re-write this part of the story from Mxolisi's point of view.

B10 An atrocious deed (chapters 11–12)

Comprehension

1 Read chapters 11–12 and tick the correct answer in the table below. Only one answer is correct for each item.

a In her community, Mandisa feels …

- **A** like the mother of a hero.
- **B** like a subject of hatred.
- **C** respected by her neighbours.
- **D** angry.

b Looking at the older generation, Mxolisi has always known that …

- **A** he is going to have a bright future.
- **B** he can get a good job by working hard.
- **C** he must attend school regularly.
- **D** he does not have any job prospects.

c When the white girl enters Guguletu in her Mazda and the mob realizes there is a white person inside …

- **A** the angry crowd stops it and people throw stones at the car.
- **B** a violent mob yells at her but lets her pass.
- **C** she is fatally hit by a stone.
- **D** her black friends attack the rioters.

d When the car is immobilized and they get out of the car, …

- **A** they manage to get to the safety of a nearby gas station.
- **B** the white girl's black friends plead with the crowd to save her.
- **C** the white girl is shot.
- **D** the angry youths stab the white girl and two of her friends.

e In the end, the rioting young people …

- **A** calm down.
- **B** burn the car but let the white girl get away.
- **C** stab the white girl.
- **D** kidnap the white girl.

Beyond the text

2 **Writing** Choose one of the following assignments.
- **a** At the police station, one of the white girl's black friends needs to give her witness statement. Write the statement from her point of view.
- **b** Take the point of view of one of the young black men and write his interior monologue (→ Info box, p. 173) about the riot and the murder.

3 **Speaking** Write down 5 questions you want to ask Mxolisi about his life and the fatal riots that led to the death of the innocent white girl. Then choose someone to take the role of Mxolisi. Take turns asking and answering your questions.

B11 Characterization

Analysis

1 **a** Form groups of three. Compare your notes about the main characters of the novel (**B2**, p. 139). Add any missing information to your lists.
- **b** Choose one of the main characters of the novel (Mandisa, Mxolisi, the white girl). Use your information from **B2** (p. 139) and write a characterization (→ Info box). The tips in the boxes below can help you.
- **c** In your group read out your characterization and listen to you partners reading theirs. Discuss what you liked about them and/or how they could be improved.

Info Writing a characterization

Collect all necessary information on the character:
personal information · appearance · family background · relationship with other characters · behaviour · thoughts and attitudes.

- **A** Start with an introduction in which you briefly introduce the character.
- **B** For the main body of the text use paragraphs to organize your thoughts. Describe the outward appearance and give background information first before you examine the character's attitudes. Use examples/quotes from the novel to analyse your character.
- **C** Write a conclusion to sum up your text.

Language help

- Use the **simple present** when you analyse a fictional text like *Mother to Mother*, even though the plot takes place at different times in Mandisa's life.
  At the age of 9, Mandisa's family is forced to move to Guguletu.
  As a teenager, Mandisa marries her boyfriend, China.
  When Mxolisi is 20 years old, he still attends sixth grade at school.
- Use suitable adjectives to describe your character:
  calm · sincere · sensible · hot-headed · diligent · lazy · energetic · conscientious · eager · careless · reliable · thoughtful · irresponsible · dutiful · inspiring · confident · cautious · polite · helpful · malicious · confused · prejudiced · troublesome · intolerant · popular · sympathetic · ruthless · honest · apologetic · ill-mannered · impatient
- You can use some of these phrases for your text:
  this behaviour reveals that · it is obvious · it indicates his/her · the way he/she is depicted/portrayed · this is a typical example of · it is also the reason why · another significant trait · this trait manifests itself when · an essential component of his/her character is · during the novel he/she undergoes a striking development

Beyond the text

2 a Work with a partner. One of you is a journalist and wants to interview Mandisa, Mxolisi or the white girl. Choose one of the following situations in the novel and prepare at least 5 questions.

Mandisa	Mxolisi	The white girl
– the forced relocation – police brutality – life in the township – ethnic diversity: Mrs. Nelson's life	– police brutality (e.g. Mzama and Zazi) – the COSAS riots – life in Guguletu – Bantu education	– working and studying in Cape Town

b Speaking With your partner, act out the interview.

Part C
Post-reading activities

C1 The real case: The murder of Amy Biehl

1 **Mediation** As an exchange student in London you are participating in a school project about South Africa. You have come across this article on the murder of Amy Biehl. For your research paper, summarize Linda Biehl's reasons for working with the people who murdered her daughter.

Der Mörder meiner Tochter und ich

Christian Putsch

[...] Ntobeko Peni trägt ein gebügeltes Hemd. Die Schuhe sind geputzt, Gesicht und Kopf ordentlich rasiert. Ein Mann, der signalisieren will: Ich habe mein Leben unter Kontrolle. [...] Doch die Schreie kommen zurück, Panische Blicke einer jungen Frau. Ihre letzten, sie blieben für immer in seinem Kopf. Peni lächelt nicht. 18 Jahre sind vergangen, seit Südafrika am Rande eines Bürgerkrieges stand und Peni zum Mörder wurde. Er marschierte an der Spitze einer Gruppe von 50 Anhängern des Panafrikanischen Kongresses (PAC). Ihr Ziel: Chaos. [...] „Zerstört Symbole der Apartheid", lautete die Ansage der PAC-Aktivisten. Dazu zählten ausdrücklich auch Menschen. [...]

Die Sonne war schon untergegangen. [...] Amy Biehl bog in ihrem klapprigen Toyota um die Ecke. Alles andere als ein Symbol der Apartheid: Eine 26-jährige Amerikanerin, die bei der Feier zu ihrem Universitätsabschluss eine Kappe mit der Aufschrift „Befreit Mandela" getragen hatte und in Kapstadt an dem neuen Wählerregister mitarbeitete. Im Auto waren drei dunkelhäutige Kolleginnen, die sie an diesem kalten Winterabend im August 1993 nach Hause fahren wollte. „Wir haben nur ihre Hautfarbe gesehen", sagt Peni, der schon als Jugendlicher der Umgang mit Waffen beigebracht worden war. Weiß, das genügte. Amy Biehl stürzte aus dem umstellten und mit Steinen beworfenen Auto, die Kolleginnen flehten vergebens: „Sie ist eine von uns." [...] Sie starb durch mehrere Messerstiche – einer traf das Herz. [...]

Linda Biehl, Amys Mutter, sitzt in einem Büro im siebten Stockwerk eines Kapstädter Hochhauses. [...] An der Wand hängen Dutzende Fotos und Malereien von Kindern aus Gugulethu, kleine Notizen von über einem Jahrzehnt Sozialarbeit der Amy-Biehl-Stiftung. Es klopft an der Tür. Peni tritt herein, sein Büro ist direkt nebenan. Er erinnert sie, dass sie sich nach dem Interview noch über eines der Jugendprogramme unterhalten müssten. [...]

Nur wenige haben verstanden, warum sie jemanden in ihre Nähe ließ, der die Zukunft ihrer Tochter zerstörte. Mehr noch – ihm sogar half, eine Zukunft aufzubauen. Peni war 1994 mit drei anderen Aktivisten zu 27 Jahren Haft für den Mord an Amy Biehl verurteilt worden.

Vier Jahre später wurde er von der Wahrheits- und Versöhnungskommission begnadigt, die zur Aufarbeitung von Verbrechen während der Apartheid eingerichtet worden war. Linda und ihr Mann Peter hatten vor Ort ausgesagt – und sich für eine Freilassung eingesetzt. Mehr noch: Peni arbeitet inzwischen für die Amy-Biehl-Stiftung, zusammen mit Easy Nofemela, der ebenfalls für das Verbrechen verurteilt worden war. [...]

„Meine Trauer ist nicht in Worte zu fassen. Wir hatten Wut in uns, aber wir haben mit dem Mord zunächst keine Individuen, sondern einen anonymen Mob in Verbindung gebracht. […]“

Vor allem aber war den Biehls bewusst, wie entscheidend jene Monate vor den Wahlen 1994 für Südafrika waren. […] Südafrikanische Rechtsextremisten kontaktierten die Biehls, um den Tod ihrer Tochter für ihre Propaganda auszuschlachten. „Die südafrikanische Demokratie war gefährdet, und damit auch ein Stück weit der Traum unserer Tochter. Wir wollten dabei helfen, beides am Leben zu erhalten.“ […]

Peni griff zum Telefon und tat das Unwahrscheinlichste, was ein Mörder von der Familie seines Opfers erwarten kann: Er bat um Hilfe. Doch Peter Biehl, Lindas Mann, sagte ein Treffen zu. Aber nicht im Büro. Er bestand darauf, nach Gugulethu zu kommen.

„Ich dachte, da ist ein Vater, der Amok laufen will“, sagt Peni, „das hätte ich zumindest getan, wenn ich an seiner Stelle gewesen wäre.“ […] Doch die Biehls kamen nicht, um zu töten. Sie wollten schaffen. […] „Wir wussten, dass Bildung und Perspektive die einzige Antwort sein kann, um derartige Verbrechen zu verhindern“, sagt Linda Biehl, „und wir hatten gesagt, unser Angebot allen zu öffnen. Daran haben wir uns gehalten.“ […]

Studien belegen, dass Gesellschaften mit hohen sozialen Unterschieden besonders für Verbrechen anfällig sind. Und beides trifft auf Südafrika, wo, proportional zur Einwohnerzahl gerechnet, 45 Mal so viele Morde wie in Deutschland passieren. Noch immer gibt es Morde durch Mobs in den Townships, die Aggressionen richten sich inzwischen auf Einwanderer aus anderen afrikanischen Ländern, die mit Südafrikanern um einfache Jobs konkurrieren. […]

Aus: Der Mörder meiner Tochter und ich *(17. Oktober 2011), Die Welt (Ausland) online*

2 **Speaking** Form groups of 3 to 5 students. Discuss whether you support the Biehl family's approach. Do you think you could act similarly if your loved one had been murdered?

C2 Justice and accountability

Comprehension

1 The concepts of 'justice' and 'accountability' are of major importance in the novel *Mother to Mother*.

a Explain both words in English. If necessary, you can use a monolingual English dictionary.

b Look at the picture of Justitia on the right. Explain why she is depicted with scales and a blindfold.

c Think of situations in which justice and accountability play a role and discuss them with a partner. Refer to texts read and films watched in class.

Analysis

2 a Describe the cartoon and analyse its message. Would this be an appropriate statement for a lawyer to make in court?

b Writing Write a short comment discussing the concepts of 'innocent' and 'guilty' from a legal, as opposed to a moral point of view.

"Could my client be innocent? Probably not. My point is it's interesting to think about."

Beyond the text

3 Read your notes about the Truth and Reconciliation Commission (**A2**, **1E**, p. 138).

a Explain why Mxolisi Ntloko's crime is eligible for a hearing by the Truth and Reconciliation Commission.

b Discuss whether you support the idea of reconciling the country by granting amnesty to people who have committed politically motivated crimes.

c Writing Write a letter to Desmond Tutu, the former head of the Truth and Reconciliation Commission. Comment on the decision to grant amnesty to Amy Biehl's murderers. Do you agree with it?

4 Accountability

a Together with a partner, list the hardships Mandisa and Mxolisi endure in their lives.

b For each aspect, decide who is responsible:
- Mandisa/Mxolisi,
- another character and/or group of people
- the apartheid government.

c **Think:** Taking all information into account, think about whether Mxolisi is a murderer or rather a victim of his environment and personal circumstances.

d Speaking **Pair:** Discuss your opinion with a partner.

e Speaking **Share**: Work with another pair. Present your ideas to each other.

C3 Quotes

1 Read the quotes below.

a Choose three of the quotes and illustrate …
… how they can be used to describe a situation or incident in the novel Mother to Mother.
OR
… how they can be used to describe the real story of Amy Biehl's murder and her parents' approach to coming to terms with the tragedy in their lives.

b Compare your results with a partner.

c **Writing** Pick your favourite quote. Using it as a starting point, write a book review of Mother to Mother.

A *'No one is born hating another person because of the colour of his skin, or his background, or his religion. People must learn to hate, and if they can learn to hate, they can be taught to love.'*
(Nelson Mandela: Long Walk to Freedom*)*

B *'It is what difference we have made to the lives of others that will determine the significance of the life we lead.'* *(Nelson Mandela)*

C *'Poverty is not an accident. Like slavery and apartheid, it is man-made and can be removed by the actions of human beings.'* *(Nelson Mandela)*

D *'Education is the most powerful weapon which you can use to change the world.'*
(Nelson Mandela)

E *'No future without forgiveness.'*
(Book title by Desmond Tutu, retired black archbishop)

F *'The blacks are tired of standing at the touchlines to witness a game that they should be playing. They want to do things for themselves and all by themselves.'*
(Stephen Biko, anti-apartheid activist, murdered by the secret police in 1977)

G *'We are not fighting against people, we are fighting against a system.'*
(Oliver Tambo, anti-apartheid activist)

Module V

Frankenstein

Part A
Pre-reading activities

A1 Anticipating themes and motifs

1 **a** Look up definitions of the three words you see in the picture.
b Describe the picture and the feelings it evokes by taking colours and setting into account.
c Discuss what kinds of turning points in life the crossroads could refer to.

Language help
signpost · weather-beaten · rough · solitude · stand at / come to a crossroads · deserted · gloomy · countryside · scenery · inscription

A2 The author

1 Speaking To find out more about Mary Shelley and *Frankenstein's* biographical background, have a look at her 'Introduction' to the novel (pp. 9–16 of the Cornelsen edition) and the short additional text about her life (pp. 276–277). Present your findings to your class.

Mary Wollstonecraft Shelley (1797–1851)

A3 Working with words

1 Fill in the gaps. Use a collocations dictionary if you need help (you can find free versions online).

Frankenstein and its historical background

The Romantic era, which started in the late 18th century and continued into the middle of the 19th century, was a time when profound changes took place in British society. Modern technologies had paved the way for the Industrial Revolution and (**A**) ________________ a significant threat to the livelihoods of many of the lower classes. The French Revolution had (**B**) ________________ the established order and an increased awareness of social injustice had developed.

Mary Shelley's time was (**C**) ________________ by social and political upheaval, but also by significant scientific developments which added to the understanding of the origins of life and the laws of nature. Some scientists suggested that chemistry might provide the secret of creating life, and discoveries were (**D**) ________________ that proved that human respiration needed oxygen produced by plants.

Many people, however, were reluctant to (**E**) ________________ that human life hinged on the vegetative world. They still believed that man's position in the world was (**F**) ________________ and that only God was able to create life and the immortal soul. It is specifically Galvanism to which Mary Shelley (**G**) ________________ in *Frankenstein*. In 1791, Luigi Galvani (**H**) ________________ a paper that dealt with 'animal electricity'. According to Galvani, this electricity was conducted by the nerves and produced muscular motion. Experiments on corpses were (**I**) ________________ to prove his theory.

As a consequence of this social and scientific progress, the Romantic literary and artistic movement focused on the individual and her/his intensive emotions, the power of imagination and creation and the (**J**) ________________ the grandeur of the natural world – all themes that are present in *Frankenstein*.

Part B
While-reading activities

B1 Walton's letters

Comprehension

1 Read the passages indicated in brackets and fill in the answers.

A Letters I–IV
Name the three locations from which Walton writes his four letters to his sister.

1 ______________________

2 ______________________

3 ______________________

B Letter I (p. 20, l. 8–p. 21, l. 18)
Complete the three motives Walton gives for his ambition to explore the 'country of eternal light'.

Revealing ______________________

Setting ______________________

Discovering ______________________

C Letter I (p. 21, l. 19–p. 23, l. 5)
Name activities and events from Walton's past that prepared him for becoming the leader of an expedition in his later life.

As a young child, he ______________________

____

'6 years ago', he ______________________

____

D Letter II (p. 26, ll. 10–21)
How did Walton's master show 'gentleness' and 'mildness' before their expedition?

____

____

____

____

E Letter IV (p. 32, l. 3–p. 34, l. 9)
Which events take place on these dates?

July 31st, 17–

____

August 1st, 17–

____

F Letter IV (p. 36, l. 14–p. 40, l. 22)
Which hints are given about Victor Frankenstein's background?

____

____

____

Analysis

2 Read the info box on atmosphere and clarify possible questions in class.

Info Atmosphere

Atmosphere is a kind mood of that literary texts convey to their readers. It is influenced by such elements as **the setting (A)**, **the depiction of characters (B)** and **other stylistic features used by the author (C** and **D)**.

A **The setting** is the background against which an action takes place. This includes
- the location, the scenery, the weather, and important objects,
- the time (historical time, time of day, season), and
- the general situation of the characters (e. g. their social situation, living conditions, etc.).

B **The depiction of the characters** adds to the atmosphere because information given in the text about their background, behaviour, language and/or interaction with each other has an effect on the reader.

C **Language-related features** such as the choice of words and literary means such as metaphor, contrast, hyperbole, alliteration, parallelism and other devices have an impact on atmosphere.

D **References to past events and foreshadowing** (i. e. hints at what might happen in the future) have an effect on atmosphere as well.
Many of these elements will reveal something about the narrator's emotional and intellectual situation (his 'mood'). Note, however, that atmosphere refers to the impact the text has on the reader.

3 **a** Elements **A** to **D** are assigned evenly to the students in class.
b Read the indicated passages from the novel and fill in the grid below.

A Setting
1. p. 20, ll. 8–18 ('… perpetual splendour')
2. p. 28, ll. 3–12
3. p. 30, ll. 3–15
4. p. 32, ll. 6–11

B Depiction of characters
1. p. 21, l. 19–p. 22, l. 7
2. p. 25, ll. 1–7; p. 26, l. 10–p. 28, l. 2
3. p. 34, l. 28–p. 35, l. 27
4. p. 38, l. 19–p. 39, l. 2

C Vocabulary and literary means
1. p. 20, ll. 3–7 *(example)*
2. p. 21, l. 19–p. 22, l. 7
3. p. 25, l. 8–p. 26, l. 9
4. p. 28, l. 13–p. 29, l. 12
5. p. 33, l. 28–p. 34, l. 9

D References to past events, foreshadowing
1. p. 20, l. 18 ('There – for with your leave …')–p. 21, l. 18
2. p. 21, l. 19–p. 22, l. 16
3. p. 36, l. 20–p. 38, l. 8
4. p. 39, l. 4–p. 40, l. 7

Example:
Your element: C **Passage:** 1

Quote(s): rejoice – evil forebodings – increasing confidence in success

Feature(s): choice of words, contrast

Effect on the reader: conveys the narrator's optimistic mood; narrator seems likable because he cares for his sister; contrast between negative and positive words creates suspense

Your element: ______ **Passage:** ______

Quote(s): ____

Feature(s): ____

____

Effect on the reader: ____

____

____

Your element: ______ **Passage:** ______

Quote(s): ____

Feature(s): ____

____

Effect on the reader: ____

____

____

Your element: ______ **Passage:** ______

Quote(s): ____________________

Feature(s): ____________________

____

Effect on the reader: ____________________

____

Your element: ______ **Passage:** ______

Quote(s): ____________________

Feature(s): ____________________

____

Effect on the reader: ____________________

____

c Compare your notes with students who worked on the same passage and category. Complete your notes and change them if necessary.

d Present your results to one student from each of the other three groups. Note down their results on a separate sheet of paper.

4 In class, find four suitable adjectives from the word banks below to describe the overall atmosphere in the first part of the novel. Then, write down three sentences using these adjectives.

alarming · barren · cold · confining · desolate · gloomy · haunting · hopeless · hostile · lonely · merciless · pessimistic · tense · uncanny · uneasy · violent · threatening

confident · ecstatic · idyllic · inclusive · joyous · liberating · light-hearted · nostalgic · vivacious · warm · welcoming

Beyond the text

5 **Writing** Imagine you are a low-ranking mate on board Walton's ship. Write a diary entry in which you express your thoughts about your captain, life on board, and the strange new passenger. Also explain what made you join the expedition in the first place.

B2 Creation (chapters 1–8)

Comprehension

1 For each chapter, tick the statement that is **not** true, underline the wrong part and correct it.

Chapter 1

A Victor's father Alphonse becomes his mother Caroline's protector after her father, Alphonse's longtime friend Beaufort, died in poverty.

B Alphonse, Caroline and their children travel extensively through Europe after their wedding.

C When Victor is about five years old, Caroline discovers the impoverished Elizabeth, who is supposedly the daughter of an aristocrat, on a trip through Italy.

Chapter 2

A Victor enjoys a pleasurable childhood, however, in retrospect, he sees his impending doom deeply rooted in certain activities and interests he started pursuing at an early age.

B Victor spends a lot of time with Elizabeth and his energetic friend Henry, as well as studying books written by scientists who are long dead.

C A modern natural philosopher accompanying the Frankenstein family explains to Victor the workings of electricity, thus supporting the metaphysicians' theories about it.

In chapter 3, Victor …

A attributes his mother's death to her previous carelessness.

B finds Professor Krempe revolting in looks, voice and behaviour. However, Krempe manages to convince him of the benefits of modern natural sciences.

C finds out that Professor Waldmann, an expert on chemistry, shows a certain admiration even for scientists whose assumptions have been proved wrong.

Chapter 4

A Victor earns esteem at the university, e. g. by improving some of the instruments used there.

B Victor is obsessed with science and overcoming death.

C As the completion of his work nears, Victor longs for rest and relaxation.

Chapter 5

- **A** When Victor looks down on the creature, he admires its perfection and beauty until it starts producing a sound.
- **B** Finding the creature standing next to his bed, Victor rushes out of his apartment and ends up pacing around a small courtyard.
- **C** During a months-long nervous fever, Victor talks to Henry Clerval about what he has done.

In chapter 6, Victor's activities include …

- **A** … introducing Henry Clerval to his professors and enjoying the study of languages from the Middle and Far East.
- **B** … going on walking tours through the vicinity of Ingolstadt.
- **C** … heading back to Geneva in late autumn.

Chapter 7

- **A** Elizabeth feels responsible for William's death and blames herself for not having watched him more closely.
- **B** To his bewildered brother Ernest, Victor expresses his doubts about whether the creature was really arrested.
- **C** Elizabeth, Victor and Alphonse are convinced of Justine Moritz's innocence.

In chapter 8, Justine Moritz …

- **A** … describes how she had to spend the night outdoors.
- **B** … is forced into a false confession of her guilt after the trial.
- **C** … is calm even in the face of her execution, expecting to go to Heaven.

2 Draw a family tree of the Frankenstein family. In a different colour, add past or present close family friends or acquaintances. Complete the diagram while finishing the novel.

Analysis

3 Think about the four themes given below and their impact on the development of young Victor's personality (as revealed in chapters 1 and 2). Then, get together in pairs and discuss which of the four had the strongest influence on young Victor. Finally, share your results in class.

Victor's interests

Place of residence

Parents/Upbringing

Elizabeth and Henry Clerval

4 Write down one sentence summing up your impression of Victor Frankenstein's character during his time as a student in Ingolstadt.

5 a Work with a partner. Make sure you know the meaning of the words in the box below and note down the corresponding nouns.

Example: affable – *affability*

ambitious – ____________	motivated – ____________
benevolent – ____________	narcissistic – ____________
determined – ____________	obsessed – ____________
driven – ____________	reckless – ____________
eager – ____________	self-assured – ____________
insane – ____________	self-aware – ____________
inspired – ____________	sinister – ____________

b Reread the following passages from the novel. Choose adjectives from the box above (or possibly others) to characterize Victor Frankenstein's thoughts and behaviour. Explain your choice.

Chapter 3
p. 61, ll. 17–26

Chapter 4
p. 65, l. 20–p. 66, l. 25

Chapter 5
p. 68, l. 24–p. 69, l. 29

6 From chapter 1, Victor Frankenstein is the *first-person narrator* of the story. Read these four passages from the novel and examine how the narrator / Victor conveys his story to his readers (→ Info box, p. 29).

A Chapter 2: p. 54, ll. 1–13	**C** Chapter 4: p. 67, ll. 17–26
B Chapter 4: p. 66, l. 26–p. 67, l. 2	**D** Chapter 8: p. 104, l. 24–p. 105, l. 7

7 Look up the meaning of the following ideas from narratology. Then, choose one of the passages from **7** to provide an example for each of these ideas. Take notes.

retrospection | addressee | obstrusiveness | (un)reliability | limitedness

8 In class, comment on the effect that Victor's narrative perspective has on the reader.

Beyond the text

9 Design a poster about Victor Frankenstein containing bullet points and some graphic illustrations surrounding the centre to visualize the different (historical, social, biographical) facets of Victor's character. Then, fill the centre of your poster with your assessment of Victor. Before you start, find out more about the Prometheus myth and Shelley's times. Reread text A3 and study the additional texts on pp. 263–268 of the Cornelsen edition of *Frankenstein*, and use the internet.
In a gallery walk, present your posters to the rest of the class.

10 **Mediation** You are taking part in an upcoming highschool Model United Nations. In the course of your conference preparations, you come across He Jiankui, a Chinese biophysicist imprisoned in December 2019 for manipulating the human genome. Write an email to the chairperson of your committee in which you strongly advocate to put the issue 'Genetic Engineering of Human Embryos' on the conference's agenda. Make use of the information provided in the article below and focus on He Jiankui's experiment, his justification for his actions as well as the dangers, and the accusations brought against him by others.

Ein Mann spielt Gott

Christoph Giesen / Kathrin Zinkant

Der Mann lässt auf sich warten. „Wenn Sie mich hören können, kommen Sie bitte auf die Bühne", sagt Robin Lovell-Badge, Professor für Entwicklungsbiologe am Francis Crick Institute in London. […] Dann endlich öffnet sich die Tür neben der Bühne, und er wieselt herein, fast schüchtern. […]

Ein kurzes Händeschütteln, dann geht er zum Pult, schaut sich um. […]

[Er] stellt brav seine Aktentasche neben das Pult, faltet umständlich einen Zettel auf. Und hetzt dann wie ein Getriebener durch seinen Vortrag. Redet von HIV, von Todesraten, von Mäuseversuchen, Affenexperimenten, Allelen, Genen. Hinter ihm hängt ein Werbebanner der Veranstaltung: „Human Genome Editing".

He Jiankui. So heißt der Mann, den bis vor Kurzem kaum jemand kannte. Er ist über Nacht berühmt geworden. Am Montag, genau einen Tag bevor die wichtigste Konferenz der Branche in Hongkong anfing, lud er bei Youtube drei Videos hoch, gefilmt in seinem Labor im chinesischen Shenzhen. He spricht in holprigem Englisch von Lulu und Nana, von Grace und Mark. Von einer glücklichen Familie, wie er sagt, dank ihm. Grace und Mark, das sind die Pseudonyme der Eltern. Lulu und Nana sind die Zwillinge, geboren vor wenigen Tagen, sie sollen die ersten Kinder sein, deren Gene verändert worden sind. Der Vater ist mit HIV infiziert, He manipuliert das Erbgut so, dass die Babys gegen das Virus immun sind, sagt er.

In den Videos erzählt He schwer gerührt von seinem Werk und von der Idee, benachteiligten Familien geholfen zu haben, er redet von der Gnade und dem Respekt für die Autonomie des Kindes. Er redet von der Verantwortung, einem Kind einen möglichst gesunden Start ins Leben zu ermöglichen. Unter gesund versteht He hier die Immunität gegen das HI-Virus, denn das ist die genetische Veränderung, die er eingefügt hat. Letztlich redet er von sich, von He, dem Schöpfer.

Und das alles, obwohl die Babys nicht einmal einer besonderen Ansteckungsgefahr ausgesetzt waren. Die genetische Veränderung von Lulu und Nana aber ist ein gewaltiger Eingriff. Sie hat beide Babys einer großen Gefahr ausgesetzt, die Genschere könnte irgendwo im Erbgut Schäden anrichten, die nie mehr rückgängig gemacht werden können und vielleicht in Jahren zu schweren Krankheiten führen. […]

Für die Wissenschaftler, die in Hongkong eigentlich über ethisch begründete Zurückhaltung reden wollten, sind He Jiankui und die zwei Kinder die größtmögliche Katastrophe. Alle hier wissen, dies ist ein Menschenversuch, bei dem ohne Skrupel schlimme Folgen für die Kinder in Kauf genommen wurden. Und: Es ist ein Experiment, durch das eines der Lieblingswerkzeuge der Wissenschaft in Verruf geraten könnte. He hat es einfach genutzt. Letztlich war es eine Frage der Zeit, bis einer es wagt.

Das Werkzeug heißt Crispr-Cas9, verkürzt sagen viele Crispr, es wurde vor fünf Jahren entdeckt und ist in der Lage, winzigste, punktgenaue Veränderungen im Erbgut aller Lebewesen einzuführen. Veränderungen, die sich von natürlichen Mutationen nicht unterscheiden. Erbanlagen können mit Crispr eingeschaltet oder ausgeschaltet werden, man kann einzelne Buchstaben oder Worte im Text des Lebens redigieren. Deshalb spricht man auch vom Gene Editing. Ob Pflanze oder Tier, Ratte oder Mensch, das Editieren funktioniert in jedem lebendigen Organismus. Es war immer klar, dass man es hier nicht nur mit einem nützlichen Werkzeug zu tun hat. Sondern auch mit einer Gefahr.

„Don't edit the Human Germline", verändert nicht die menschliche Keimbahn, forderte eine Gruppe von Wissenschaftlern vor drei Jahren in Science, einem der angesehensten Wissenschaftsjournale. Es war ein Aufruf zur Selbstbeschränkung, zur Besonnenheit, und der erste öffentliche Hinweis darauf, dass ein ethischer Dammbruch drohen könnte. Initiiert hatte den Artikel eine der Erfinderinnen der Genschere, die amerikanische Chemikerin Jennifer Doudna von der University of California in Berkeley. […]

Der Forscherin war bewusst, dass ihre Genschere auch im ganz frühen menschlichen Embryo eingesetzt werden könnte, gleich nach der Befruchtung. Zu diesem Zeitpunkt besteht der Mensch aus einer einzigen Zelle, alle anderen gehen aus ihr hervor, auch der männliche Samen oder die weiblichen Eizellen.

Verändert man also gleich nach der Befruchtung etwas im Embryo, wird diese Veränderung auf alle folgenden Generationen übertragen. Was man getan hat, geht nicht mehr weg. Es ist ein Eingriff in die Evolution. Würde ihn jemand wagen, zum Beispiel, um erbliche Krankheiten für immer aus der Spezies Mensch zu eliminieren?

Nicht nur Doudna war bei dem Gedanken extrem unwohl, zahlreiche namhafte Experten schlossen sich ihr an. Sie wussten, dass die Genschere bei all ihren großartigen Eigenschaften nicht frei von Fehlern ist, sie schneidet manchmal an Stellen, an denen das nicht vorgesehen ist. Das ist extrem riskant, wichtige Erbanlagen können verändert werden, schwere Krankheiten wären die Folge. „Bevor – und wenn überhaupt – Versuche zum Gene Editing in Menschen gebilligt werden können, müssen die möglichen Sicherheits- und Wirksamkeitsaspekte dieser Technologie sorgfältig untersucht und auch verstanden werden", schrieben die Crispr-Fachleute schon damals. Daran hat sich bis heute wenig geändert. Crispr ist für einen Einsatz im Embryo nicht sicher. Völlig abgesehen von der Frage, was man denn am Menschen ändern darf.

Nach Hes Vortrag kommt David Baltimore auf die Bühne. Er ist so etwas wie der Doyen der Gentechnik, 1975 hat er den Nobelpreis bekommen. Das Experiment sei unverantwortlich, sagt er. „Ich denke nicht, dass es medizinisch notwendig gewesen ist. Es handelt sich um ein Versagen der Selbstregulierung unserer Gemeinschaft." [...]

Kommunikativ ist der Coup jedenfalls durchdacht und bestens geplant. Es gibt eine eigene Webseite, einen Youtube-Kanal, offenbar auch ein Exklusivabkommen mit bestimmten Medien. Hes Vortrag steht wenige Minuten, nachdem er beendet ist, schon im Internet.

Dann kommen Lovell-Badge und sein Fachkollege Matthew Porteus aus Stanford auf die Bühne. Porteus fragt: „Nennen Sie uns bitte die Zahlen. Wie viele Paare, wie viele Embryos, wie viele Kinder?" Es seien zunächst acht Paare gewesen, sagt He. Alle Väter seien HIV-positiv, die Mütter negativ. Ein Paar habe sich entschieden auszusteigen. Mehr als 30 Embryonen, sagt er, hätten sich „weiterentwickelt". „Gibt es noch weitere Schwangerschaften?", fragt Porteus.

„Es gibt noch einen anderen potenziellen Fall", sagt He.

Vielleicht gibt es also bald noch mehr Kinder, die He Jiankui erschaffen hat. [...]

Ein Professor der Peking-Universität meldet sich zu Wort: „Es gibt unter chinesischen Wissenschaftlern eine klare Vereinbarung, dass wir nicht an Menschen forschen", sagt er. „Warum haben Sie die klinischen Studien heimlich durchgeführt?"

„Die Leute brauchen Hilfe. Wir haben die Technologie dazu, also sollten wir ihnen auch helfen", sagt He.

Viele chinesische Wissenschaftler distanzieren sich von Hes Forschung, 120 haben einen offenen Brief geschrieben, nachdem bekannt wurde, was da in Shenzhen gemacht worden war. [...]

Die letzte Frage, die auf dem Podium gestellt wird, ist folgende: „Wenn es um Ihre eigenen Kinder gegangen wäre, wären Sie das Risiko eingegangen?"

Kurze Pause, dann sagt He: „Ich hätte es versucht." Dann nimmt er seine Aktentasche und verschwindet, beinahe so plötzlich, wie er gekommen ist.

From: Ein Mann spielt Gott, *Süddeutsche Zeitung, 29. November2018*

B3 Development (chapters 9–17)

Comprehension

1 Match the following summaries to chapters 9–17 and fill in the missing parts.

A The monster speaks to the old De Lacey. The latter promises to help him, and the monster grabs De Lacey's hand in gratitude. Just then, the others return from a walk and Felix

____.

B Observing the poor people in the cottage, the monster learns some simple words and understands the meaning of true compassion. The monster does little jobs for them to

____.

C The monster seeks Victor in Geneva. It takes him the better part of a year to travel to the city after nearly being killed when ______________________________ and killing William, Victor's youngest brother.

D On the slopes of the Mer de Glace glacier, the monster attacks Victor and persuades him to visit his hut to ____________________________________.

E The monster tells Victor about how he was beaten and chased away, and then learned to survive by foraging in a forest and by living in a ________________________.

F The monster urges Victor to create a female companion for him so he would not be alone any longer. He promises that they would flee to ________________________.

G The monster learns about the story of Safie's family and the De Laceys' part in it. The De Laceys are forced to live in exile in Germany because ____________________

____.

H Victor decides to go to nearby Chamonix Valley, known for its natural beauty and soothing scenery. There, he is finally able to find relief, and manages to

____.

I Eavesdropping on Felix reading from a book to newly-arrived Safie and observing the cottagers, the monster learns about men, women, and families. He is haunted by the question ____.

Chapter	9	10	11	12	13	14	15	16	17

Analysis

2 a Before reading the following text, talk with a partner about traits that are exclusively attributed to humans.

b Compare your results in class.

The traits that make human beings unique

Melissa Hogenboom

[...] Ever since we learned to write, we have documented how special we are. The philosopher Aristotle marked out our differences over 2,000 years ago. We are 'rational animals' pursuing knowledge for its own sake. We live by art and reasoning, he wrote.

Much of what he said stills stands. Yes, we see the roots of many behaviours once considered uniquely human in our closest relatives, chimpanzees and bonobos. But we are the only ones who peer into their world and write books about it.

[...] 'The Neanderthals had an impressive but basically routine material record for a hominid. Once *H. sapiens* started behaving in a strange, [more sophisticated] way, all hell broke loose and change became the norm,' [paleoanthropologist Ian] Tattersall says. We started to produce superior cultural and technological artefacts. Our stone tools became more intricate. One study proposes that our technological innovation was key for our migration out of Africa. We started to assign symbolic values to objects such as geometrical designs on plaques and cave art.

By contrast, there is little evidence that any other hominins made any kind of art. One example, which was possibly made by Neanderthals, was hailed as proof they had similar levels of abstract thought. However, it is a simple etching and some question whether Neanderthals made it at all. The symbols made by *H. sapiens* are clearly more advanced. We had also been around for 100,000 years before symbolic objects appeared so what happened?

Somehow, our language-learning abilities were gradually 'switched on', Tattersall argues. In the same way that early birds developed feathers before they could fly, we had the mental tools for complex language before we developed it.

We started with language-like symbols as a way to represent the world around us, he says. For example, before you say a word, your brain first has to have a symbolic representation of what it means. These mental symbols eventually led to language in all its complexity and the ability to process information is the main reason we are the only hominin still alive, Tattersall argues.

It's not clear exactly when speech evolved, or how. But it seems likely that it was partly driven by another uniquely human trait: our superior social skills.

Comparative studies between humans and chimps show that while both will cooperate, humans will always help more. Children seem to be innate helpers. They act selflessly before social norms set in. Studies have shown that they will spontaneously open doors for adults and pick up 'accidentally' dropped items. They will even stop playing to help. Their sense of fairness begins young. Even if an experiment is unfairly rigged so that one child receives more rewards, they will ensure a reward is fairly split.

We know that chimpanzees also work together and share food in apparently unselfish ways. However, Michael Tomasello of the Max Planck institute for Evolutionary Anthropology in Leipzig, Germany, says they will only cooperate if there is something in it for them.

'Humans do that too, but in addition they care about what their partner gets. In some experiments we have children as young as 14–18 months who seem to expect their partner to collaborate in certain ways and who share in ways chimps don't.'

Human children are less selective about who they share with. Chimpanzees though, largely only share with close relatives, reciprocating partners or potential mates.

Felix Warneken of Harvard University in Cambridge, US, differentiates it like this. Children are 'proactive', that is, they help even when presented with only very subtle cues. Chimpanzees though, need more encouragement. They are 'reactive': they will hand over objects but only after some nudging.

Something must have happened in our evolution, Tomasello says, to make humans increasingly reliant on each other. Our brains needed fuel to get bigger and so collaborative hunting may have played a key role in that. Our advanced teamwork may simply reflect our long history of working together to get food.

[...] Charles Darwin, in his book *The Descent of Man*, wrote that humans and animals only differ in degree, not kind. This still stands true but [evolutionary psychologist Thomas] Suddendorf says that it is precisely these gradual changes that make us extraordinary and has led to 'radically different possibilities of thinking'.

From: The traits that make human being unique, *BBC Future online (accessed February 21, 2020), July 6, 2015,*

3 Find headings for the paragraphs and note down qualities that are unique to man.

A ll. 1–13: ______________________________

B ll. 14–36: ______________________________

C ll. 37–55: ______________________________

D ll. 56–107: ______________________________
(two social skills)

4 Take a closer look at chapters 10–12, use ideas from tasks **2** and **3**, and analyse to what extent the creature displays human traits. Take notes in the table below.

Human trait	Evidence from the text (bullet points)	Page, lines

Beyond the text

5 **Writing** Choose one of the following tasks:

a Comment on the following question: Why does Mary Shelley use the terms *creature* or *monster* to refer to Frankenstein's creation rather than giving it a name?

b Comment on the statement by British *Frankenstein* expert Susan J. Wolfson:

> *'The dark brilliance of* Frankenstein *is both to expose "monstrosity" in the normal and, conversely, to humanize what might seem monstrously "other".'*
>
> *From: Susan Wolfson, 'A "Monster" and its humanity', Princeton Alumni Week online, 10 January 2018*

Beyond the text

6 After the monster's 'attack', the De Laceys discuss what to do next.

a Get together in groups of four and decide who is taking on the roles of De Lacey (father), Felix, Agatha and Safie.

b What stance could your character take in the discussion? Take notes considering your role's past, personality and motives.

c **Speaking** Act out the role play.

d Talk about your performances. Were the characters depicted in a convincing way?

B4 Revenge (chapters 18–24)

Comprehension

1 Follow Victor's route by putting the places below in the correct order.

Edinburgh

Oxford

Ireland

Orkneys

Rotterdam

Paris

London

Strasbourg

Geneva (2x)

Arctic Sea

____

____

2 Match the sentence beginnings with the correct endings (one ending is not needed).

A Victor Frankenstein travels to England since he

B Victor takes Clerval with him on his journey in order to

C The monster vows revenge because Victor

D In Ireland, Victor is imprisoned because he

E Back in Geneva, Elizabeth dies on their wedding night because Victor

F Victor heads off to the north

G On his deathbed, Victor makes Walton promise

H After telling Walton his side of the story, the monster departs into the darkness because it

1 cannot live with the thought of having turned into an evil being.

2 thought she was safe when she was not with him.

3 protect him from the creature.

4 to seek vengeance on the monster.

5 does not want to create the creature's companion in his family home.

6 feels badly treated by society.

7 destroyed the work he had done on a female companion for the monster.

8 to destroy the monster for good.

9 is suspected of having killed Henry Clerval.

Beyond the text

3 **Writing** Write an interior monologue in which Victor decides whether to complete the female companion for the monster, or not. Take emotions, ethical aspects, and the characters of both Victor and the monster into consideration.

Info Interior monologue
This narrative device reveals a character's inner thoughts, which may be either loosely related or more rationally structured. Writing an interior monologue, your sentence structure should reflect the character's emotional state of mind.

4 Discuss with your partner: What would have happened if Victor had not destroyed the monster's companion?

Part C
Post-reading activities

C1 Ethics of science – Genetic engineering for everyone?

1 Get together in groups of four and discuss Joseph Zayner's quotation below.

'We are at the first time in the history of humanity where we can no longer be stuck with the genes we are dealt. As a society we have begun to see how choice is a right, but for some reason when it comes to genetics, some people think we shouldn't have a choice. I can be smart and attractive, but everyone else should be ugly, fat, and short because those are the genes they were dealt and they should just deal with it.' (Josiah Zayner)

Info Josiah Zayner
Josiah Zayner is a former NASA scientist whose company *TheODIN* makes genetic engineering accessible to a lay audience. He belongs to a group of biohackers who conduct experiments on their own bodies in the hope of boosting their physical and cognitive performance. On his website, you can order gene engineering kits.

a Each of you makes a list of arguments for and against easy access to genetic engineering.
b Together, rank the arguments from most important to least important.
c In your group, discuss whether everyone should have easy access to genetic engineering. You can use proverbs and idioms from the box below to add emphasis.
d **Speaking** Present your ranking of arguments and summarize your discussion in class. Comment on the other groups' presentations and add ideas.

Language help
These proverbs and idioms might help you to express your thoughts and add emphasis to them. Use a dictionary to look up unknown words.

The road to hell is paved with good intentions.
Learn to walk before you run.
It's better to be safe than sorry.
The end justifies the means.
God helps those who help themselves.
Fortune favours the brave.
Every man is the architect of his own destiny.
Playing with fire …

C2 The role of nature – interactions

1 Work with a partner and describe one of the Romantic paintings on this page. Use the language box if you need help.

William Turner (1775–1851), Calais Pier *(1803)*

Caspar David Friedrich (1774–1840), Wanderer Above the Sea of Fog *(ca. 1817)*

Caspar David Friedrich (1774–1840), Two Men Contemplating the Moon *(ca. 1825)*

Language help

moor a boat · rope · sea foam · gale · tilted · (frock) coat · walking cane · gnarled branches · leaning tree

2 Go online and find further information about the paintings and the artistic and literary movement of Romanticism.

3 Each painting depicts man's relationship with nature. Try to characterize this relationship in one sentence.

4 Discuss which picture best describes Victor Frankenstein's interactions with nature in the course of the novel. Keep in mind that the creation of the monster can be interpreted as a serious interference with nature. Give examples from the novel.

C3 Questions of human identity: The monster – a 'social animal'?

1 a Preparation: Describe the differences between the words *loneliness, isolation, solitude* and *alienation*. Go online and search for definitions if you need help.

b Speaking Get together in groups of three or four. Talk about reasons why people might experience loneliness, isolation, solitude or alienation. Discuss in what way the terms are related.

c Discuss which of the four terms above describes the monster's condition most accurately. Consider also the reasons that lead to his situation. Create an infographic that illustrates your findings. Put your infographics on display and discuss them in class.

Info Infographics
An infographic is a visual representation of information or data. Most often, it is a collection of imagery, charts and short texts which makes abstract knowledge easy to understand.

2 Get together in groups of three to four and draw a placemat on a sheet of paper.

'I am malicious because I am miserable' (p. 174, ll. 20–21), the monster says. Being denied access to social life, the monster cannot be blamed for his reactions.

Step 1: Work alone: Comment on the statement above. Write down ideas and questions on the placemat.
Step 2: Read what your group members have written down.
Step 3: Discuss and decide whether you agree or disagree with the statement.